Communication and Language with Literacy

Brilliant
PUBLICATIONS

Irene Yates

Publisher's information

Brilliant Publications
Unit 10
Sparrow Hall Farm
Edlesborough
Dunstable, Bedfordshire
LU6 2ES

Tel: **01525 222292**
Fax: **01525 222720**
e-mail: **info@brilliantpublications.co.uk**
Website: **www.brilliantpublications.co.uk**

Written by Irene Yates
Illustrated by Charlie-Anne Turner

© Irene Yates 2003.
Revised and Updated by Debbie Chalmers 2013

Printed ISBN 978 0 85747 673 9
e-book ISBN 978 0 85747 676 0

First published in the UK in 2013.
10 9 8 7 6 5 4 3 2 1

Printed in the UK.

There are three books in the Foundation
Blocks series, each covering one of the
prime areas and one or two of the specific
areas of the *Early Years Foundation Stage*.
Each book contains a wealth of activities,
ideas and suggestions, clearly described and
illustrated. Further details on how these books
are structured and how they can make it easy
to implement the Department of Education's
new, revised *Statutory Framework for the
EYFS* (September 2012) are given in the
Introduction.

Other books in the Foundation Blocks series
are:
*Physical Development and Expressive Arts &
Design* by Maureen Warner and Mavis Brown
Encourages children to be active, move with
confidence, control and co-ordination, make
healthy lifestyle and food choices, learn to
care for personal needs, explore media and
materials, use imagination in design and
technology and share thoughts, ideas and
feelings through dance, movement, art, music
and role-play.

*Personal, Social and Emotional Development,
Understanding the World and Mathematics*
by Mavis Brown and Rebecca Taylor
Encourages children to develop self-
confidence and positive attitudes and
relationships, manage feelings and behaviour,
explore the environment and community,
investigate, experiment, begin to use
technology and develop skills in counting,
addition and subtraction, understanding
and using numbers, problem solving; and
describing shape, space and measures.

Contents

Contents continued

Contents continued

Contents continued

Contents continued

Introduction

This book has over 145 differentiated activities set in real-life contexts relevant to children in the Early Years Foundation Stage (EYFS). The activities aim to develop children's skills and to meet the Department of Education's learning and development requirements in the areas of Communication and Language and Literacy. They offer opportunities for practitioners to follow the guidance document Development Matters and to encourage and support children as they work towards the Early Learning Goals (ELGs) of the new, revised Statutory Framework for the Early Years Foundation Stage (September 2012).

There are three ELGs for the prime area Communication and Language: Listening and Attention; Understanding; and Speaking.

There are two ELGs for the prime area Literacy: Reading; and Writing.

A table showing which learning opportunities are addressed by each activity can be found on pages 190–197.

The skills that children need to use, in order to attain these ELGs by the end of the EYFS, rely on each other and work together. They continue to develop throughout our lives and are what we learn to do, rather than to know. Skills cannot be taught or learned in the same way as information. They must be learned through trying, failing, trying again, succeeding, practising and improving.

It is vital that children are given lots of opportunities to extend their listening skills. They should listen to adults and peers in familiar situations, which may be informal (times for stories, songs and rhymes), more formal (circle and discussion times), or casual (while playing, following instructions or chatting). While they are practising listening and responding to others, they are also developing and using thinking, understanding and speaking skills.

Children's thinking and understanding skills develop ahead of their speaking skills. Young children may be reluctant to put their thinking into words for fear of being 'wrong' or of being laughed at. Adults must try to ensure that all children feel comfortable about speaking aloud within a familiar group, even if they think that they might make 'mistakes'. There is no possibility of failure in communication skills, since children will use verbal and non-verbal language appropriate to the stages and levels they have reached. Children should be helped and supported while attempting to say new words, as through repeating words in appropriate contexts, the words will become part of their active vocabulary and will be available for their future use in thinking, speaking and writing.

© Irene Yates
www.brilliantpublications.co.uk

When children are working within the early stages of reading and writing, it is best for adults to act as role models and allow the children to learn new skills at their own pace. Following words from left to right with a finger while reading them demonstrates to children that, in English, words are read in that direction. Thinking aloud about the sound at the beginning of a word teaches children how they will begin to write that word.

Skills must always be developed alongside concepts and attitudes. If children are developing listening or writing skills, they must be listening to or writing about something, which will be a certain concept. They will also be applying an attitude to what they are doing. It is of vital importance that children learn good attitudes towards the things they do during the formative early years. Their play and learning activities need to be fun, interesting and challenging enough to give them the confidence and the motivation to seek out further experiences. If they enjoy the early stages of speaking, reading and writing, they will form desirable attitudes towards them which, hopefully, will continue throughout their lives.

Auditory and visual discrimination do not develop in all children at the same rate, but can greatly affect their language skills and abilities. Some children in the Foundation Stage may not yet have the ability to perceive differences between shapes of letters or to discriminate between sounds easily. This is merely a physical immaturity and, with lots of practice, they will develop these skills.

Most of the activities in this book can be adapted to fit any topic or project that is being explored by a group of children. The tasks are designed to allow practitioners to choose their own directions and to include opportunities for exploration and new challenges as children's skills are being developed.

The activities are divided into five sections to indicate which prime or specific area and which of the ELGs each one will particularly contribute to. Practitioners may use this information when planning, to ensure that they are not concentrating too much on one area at the expense of another and that they are providing enough encouragement and experiences for all children to listen, understand, speak, read and write. Some activities contribute to more than one ELG and many are also strongly linked to other learning and development areas and their ELGs. (See Table of Learning opportunities on pages 190–197.)

To avoid the clumsy 'he/she', the child is referred to throughout the book as 'she'.

Planning

Where relevant, the activities have been linked to sixteen popular topics that are frequently used in early years and primary settings. These are:

- Animals
- Colours
- Food and shopping
- Health
- Myself
- Seasons
- Toys
- Water

- Celebrations
- Families
- Gardening
- Homes
- People who help us
- Shapes
- Travel and transport
- Weather

The topic appears in a shaded box at the top of each page. The other books in this series use the same topics. However, these are only suggestions and all of the activities can easily be modified to fit with other topics.

All activities are designed with the Statutory Framework for the EYFS in mind and, therefore, link with other learning and development areas, offering opportunities to explore them all with the children. Practitioners will be aware of needing to provide a balanced curriculum and to explore, along with Communication and Language and Literacy: Physical Development, Personal, Social and Emotional Development, Mathematics, Understanding the World and Expressive Arts and Design.

Prior knowledge is not expected for any of the activities, but practitioners should use their own judgement to choose activities to suit children's developmental stages.

Although plenary sessions have not been included, practitioners will recognize the importance of reviewing activities and encouraging children to verbalize what they did, how they felt about it and what they think they achieved. It is also important, of course, to discuss with parents and carers how they might build upon the children's experiences, so that they can learn consistently in the setting and at home.

© Irene Yates
www.brilliantpublications.co.uk

Logos used on the activity sheets

Box 1 – group size
This box indicates the number of children recommended for the activity, keeping safety and level of difficulty in mind. Less able children can achieve more difficult tasks with a smaller child to adult ratio. The group size indicates the size of group for the activity itself, rather than for any introductory or plenary sessions.

Box 2 – level of difficulty
This box uses a scale between 1 and 5 to depict the level of difficulty or challenge the task might present to the children. Children still developing skills described in the 22–36 months age band of the Development Matters guidance document will find 1 most suitable, whilst 2 and 3 will apply to children as they move through the 30–50 months age band. Children just entering the 40-60+ months age band will appreciate 4, while 5 will be suitable for older and more able children who are already meeting the Early Learning Goals. As most settings have mixed age groups, the majority of the activities have been classified as easy, so that the whole group can be involved. Higher levels can be achieved for particular children, as appropriate, by encouraging them to develop their own ideas and to participate in the suggested extension activities.

Box 3 – time needed to complete the activity
The suggested time slots are only a guideline. Children need time to practise their skills, test their ideas and reflect upon their findings. Some children will wish to extend the original activity to pursue their own enquiries or improve upon their experiment.

Safety
Where relevant, additional safety notes are included on the sheets. You are advised to read these before commencing the activity.

Links to home
● The word 'parent' is used to refer to all those persons responsible for the child, and include mothers, fathers, legal guardians and primary carers of children in public care. The 'Links to home' suggest ways in which parents can continue and reinforce the learning that is experienced at the setting.

- Parents can share important information about their children and their experiences, upon which practitioners can build. It is essential that practitioners find out from parents details of any special or additional needs, allergies, intolerances or medical conditions.

- Parents can be a valuable resource, giving support when extra help is needed during visits out of the setting, and with more complex activities during designing and making. They can become the knowledgeable visitor, bringing their own language, culture and experiences to the setting.

- Parents are also a useful source of recycled materials, which are required for many of the tasks.

Safety

- Children are active learners, and investigative, exploratory and construction activities invariably involve the use of potentially dangerous equipment. Part of the learning process involves offering the child the opportunity to learn to use this equipment safely. As young children cannot anticipate danger, practitioners have to be vigilant and take part in a regular risk assessment exercise relevant to their own setting.

- Any rules issued by your employer or LEA should be adhered to in priority to the recommendations in this book; therefore check your employer's and LEA's Health and Safety guidelines and their policies on the use of equipment.

Templates and other resources

On pages 168–176 there are photocopiable templates to be used in conjunction with relevant activities. The pieces will last longer if they are laminated.

Also included are the words to many traditional rhymes (pages 177–182) and storylines for some traditional tales (pages 183–187).

© Irene Yates
www.brilliantpublications.co.uk

Assessment

● Each activity has learning objectives which are linked to the prime area of Communication and Language and/or the specific area of Literacy.

● To assist practitioners in planning a balanced educational programme of experiences, the chart on pages 188–195 shows which activities address which of the Department of Education's EYFS Early Learning Goals.

● Comments on these activities and other evidence of children's achievements, such as dated examples of early writing, dictations, drawings, paintings and photographs of 3D models and 'work in progress', can be kept in a file or portfolio and given to parents as a celebration and record for the future.

● These records should be retained for inspection.

Communication and Language

Listening and Attention

- Playing with language, like all other types of play, has great power and can provide children with excellent opportunities for developing the skills of communication. Listening to others and taking part in conversations that interest them helps children to learn to focus their attention and to respond appropriately to what is said. Listening attentively to stories and rhymes helps children to understand what is real and what is nonsense and gives them opportunities to experience the pleasure and fun of using language.

- Stories, poems and nursery rhymes are important because they give the children the confidence to enjoy this kind of language play. Research has found that children who have lots of experience of stories and rhymes find learning to read easier than children who have none. This may be because they have a deeper understanding of how language works. Through learning, reciting and singing nursery rhymes, the children absorb many of the rules of speech rhythms and patterns that they will need when they start to read. They will also have a greater knowledge of the sounds of words, which makes the task of learning letters and phonics much easier. Children who can accurately anticipate or predict key events and phrases or repeated refrains in stories and rhymes are likely to be successful readers. They will also be confident communicators, able to respond to what they hear with relevant comments, questions or actions.

- Less confident children may feel able to join in with group stories, songs and rhymes. Adults can encourage this and build confidence gradually, until the children begin to speak to them, then to chat with other children and, eventually, to address the group.

- All cultures have sets of folk stories, rhymes and songs. Try to build up a large repertoire and use rhymes and songs from other cultures wherever it is possible and appropriate. Translations can be provided, but it doesn't actually matter if the children do not understand all of the words they are singing. If they are making the right pattern of sounds they are widening their language horizons.

Face to face

Learning objectives
● To develop and practise listening skills
● To give attention to what others say and respond appropriately in conversation

What to do
● During informal or formal play, try to position yourself so that children can look directly into your eyes. This is one of the simplest but most important things you can do to encourage communication. The child can then watch how your mouth forms words and watch your eyes to see what you are looking at or what feelings you are betraying.
● It is important always to talk 'with' children, not 'at' them. Let the children lead the conversation whenever possible, even when you are tempted to 'fill in' for them. If they are struggling to find the right words, prompt gently and give positive feedback as soon as they pick up the vocabulary.

Extensions/variations
● Come down to the children's level whenever they need to speak or listen to you.
● Adjust your position so that a child can see your face while sitting on your lap to talk or read stories.
● Sit with children, on the floor and at small tables, and make sure that your face is on a level with theirs while making conversation.

Links to home
● Try to use these strategies in front of parents. Explain how important they are whenever you have an opportunity.

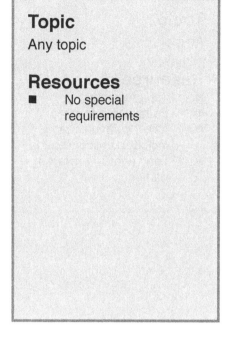

Topic
Any topic

Resources
■ No special requirements

I hear this

Topic
Animals

Resources
- Tape recorder
- Blank cassette tape
- CD or computer game including animal sounds
- Lotto and *Soundtracks* games

Learning objectives
- To show interest in and play with sounds
- To listen attentively, concentrate and respond to the sounds heard

Preparation
- Have the children sitting together, ready to listen and concentrate.

What to do
- Tell the children that you are going to play a game together called 'I hear this'.
- Explain the game – you and the children take it in turns to make a sound, and the other children have to guess what it is.
- Give an example to start – 'I hear this... moo, mooo, mooooo. What can I hear?'
- When the children have guessed it is a cow, invite them to take turns to think of more sounds, and make them for others to guess.

Extensions/variations
- Make a tape-recording of different animal sounds to play to the children, or find an appropriate CD or computer game, so that they can compare the animal sounds they make with real ones.
- Play games with small groups of children, involving listening for sounds and covering appropriate pictures on boards (such as lotto and *Soundtracks*).

Guess what?

Learning objectives
● To listen to what others say and respond appropriately
● To use descriptive vocabulary to clarify ideas

What to do
● Explain the game to the children. One player is chosen to think of an object and describe it. The others try to find out what the object is.
● Provide an example for the children by taking the first turn. For example, you could say, 'I'm thinking of something that we have in this room. You can pick it up and walk around with it. It's made of plastic. Sometimes you talk in it and sometimes you listen. The ones we have here are used in pretending games, but you might have a real one at home. The one at home will have a number. It begins with the sound 't', or sometimes the sound 'ph'. You can talk to somebody else using it.'
● When the children guess what you are thinking of, invite them to take turns to choose and describe an object for the group.

Extensions/variations
● Remind the children that they don't have to be able to *see* what they are thinking about, just give sensible clues (they might be thinking of a dinosaur, for instance).
● Let some of the children work in pairs if it makes it easier for them.

Topic
Any topic

Resources
■ Toys and other small play equipment

What can it be?

Topic
Any topic

Resources
- Tape recorder
- Blank cassette

- There is no limit to the number of sounds that children are familiar with, without ever listening to. Leave a short gap between each sound so that they don't run into each other.
- Have the children sitting together, quietly, ready to listen and concentrate.

Learning objectives
- To maintain attention, concentrate and sit quietly in order to participate
- To recognize and respond to familiar sounds
- To name and distinguish between environmental sounds

Preparation
- Use the tape recorder to record lots of different sounds, such as:
  - Washing up
  - Water running
  - Envelope opening
  - Newspaper rustling
  - Sausages frying
  - Birds singing
  - Cat meowing
  - Aeroplane going overhead
  - Cars passing
  - Bicycle bell.

What to do
- Tell the children that you are going to play a special tape to them. You want them to listen very carefully and put up their hands to speak in turn to tell you what they think each sound is. Play the first sound and pause the tape at the first gap. Invite suggestions. Rewind the tape and play the sound again. Ask the children if they have changed their minds or if they have any different ideas, or has the second hearing confirmed what they thought?
- Repeat the process with the rest of the sounds.

Extensions/variations
- Take small groups of children around your setting or local area and encourage them to listen carefully to decide which sounds to record for the rest of the group.
- Try to tape sounds that fit in with work you are doing in other areas.

What's this?

Learning objectives
● To maintain attention, concentrate and sit quietly in order to listen and participate
● To respond to sounds heard
● To confidently try a new activity and speak within a familiar group

Preparation
● Have the children sitting together, ready to listen and concentrate.

What to do
● Put all the objects on the tray and show them to the children. Get the children to identify and name them. Let them hold the objects and feel them, if they want to.
● Put something in between the children and the tray, so that they cannot see it. Ask them to close their eyes and listen carefully. Take one of the objects and drop it on to the tray from a short height.
● Ask the children to put up their hands if they think they can identify the object from the sound it makes.
● When all the objects have been dropped, remove the screen and repeat the dropping process, with the children watching and listening.

Extensions/variations
● Try using the same objects but dropping them onto something made of a different material, to find out how the sounds change.
● Drop the objects from a much greater height and decide whether this changes the sounds.
● When the children are good at the game, try dropping objects that they have not previously identified.

Topic
Sound

Resources
■ A tin tray
■ Different objects, such as keys, rubber ball, marbles, pencil, spoon, etc
■ A screen or similar

I went on a bus...

Topic
Transport and travel

Resources
■ No special requirements

Learning objectives
● To maintain concentration and follow directions
● To listen attentively to what others say and respond appropriately

Preparation
● Have the children sitting together, ready to listen and concentrate.

What to do
● This game is a variation on 'I went shopping...' in that it begins, 'I went on a bus and out of the window I saw...'. You can begin the list yourself, the child who comes next has to say your item and then choose and add an item of her own.
● The children take turns to add something they might have seen to the list, trying to remember everything that has been mentioned and not miss anything out. When the children lose track and the list breaks down, start again with someone new and a new choice.

Extensions/variations
● This game can go on for as long as you would like it to, and can be varied to fit any theme. For example:
  ◆ *For my birthday I would like...*
  ◆ *At the zoo there is a...*
  ◆ *At the toy shop I saw...*
● Play a game of things the children can do with different parts of their bodies, *I can...*

Make a call

Learning objectives
- To listen and respond to others in conversation
- To understand how to ask questions and how to reply
- To extend vocabulary through hearing and using new words
- To show interest in and model the use of technological devices

Preparation
- Have telephones and mobiles in all areas of play, including outside play, so that they are accepted as a normal part of all activities.

What to do
- Suggest scenarios in which the children might have telephone conversations with each other:
  - Friends and family: seeing how people are and arranging visits
  - Doctor and patient
  - Doctor and hospital
  - Hospital and patient
  - Emergency services: reporting a fire or an accident
  - Hairdressers: making appointments or putting appointments off
  - The vet's and a pet owner
  - The garage: to sort out a broken car
  - The booking office: booking tickets for a trip or a party
  - The supermarket: checking something is in stock
  - The travel agent: to book a holiday.
- You will notice endless opportunities whilst observing play and role-play, for the children to take on roles and have telephone conversations with each other.

Extension/variation
- Provide a tape recorder so that the children can sometimes 'formalize' their telephone conversations and record them. Ask them to listen to their recordings and find out whether they speak in a slightly different way when

Topic
People who help us

Resources
- Old telephones
- Discarded mobiles
- Tape recorder
- Blank cassette tape

they are making a recording of their own voices.

Related activity
- Taking messages (see page 164)

What does this do?

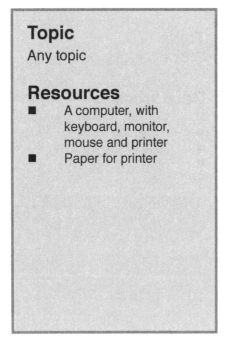

Topic
Any topic

Resources
- A computer, with keyboard, monitor, mouse and printer
- Paper for printer

Learning objectives
- To focus and maintain attention, concentrate and follow directions
- To begin to learn, remember and understand the names of different parts of a computer
- To recognize that a range of technology is used in places such as homes, schools and nurseries

What to do
- Computers and printers will be a part of children's lives, so practitioners should seek to support them in learning to identify different parts and beginning to use and understand computer vocabulary and "language"
- Ask the children if they know what kinds of things computers can do. They will have lots of different answers. Encourage discussion about any experiences they have of computers.
- Show the parts of the computer:
  - The monitor – tell them what it is called.
  - The screen switch – show them how it switches the screen on and off and let them use it.
  - The printer – ask them if they know what it does. Show them where the paper goes in and ask them if they know where it comes out.
  - The keyboard – show them the letters on the keyboard and invite them to tell you the names or sounds of any of them that they recognize.
  - The mouse – move the mouse to show them how it moves the arrow around the screen. Show the children how to click the button on the left side of the mouse.
- Suggest that you work together to open and start up a program. Decide on a program and encourage the children to help you call it up. Encourage them to use the correct words by using them yourself. Let them click on the mouse and watch the screen to see what appears. If possible, use the printer, and watch what comes out of it.

Extension/variation
- Word process a piece of creative writing and print it.

Related activity
- Send an e-mail (see page 122)

Finger rhymes

Learning objectives
● To join in with repeated refrains and fit actions to rhymes, working as a member of a group
● To enjoy rhyming and rhythmic activities and to recognize rhythm in spoken words
● To develop control and coordination in large and small movements
● To create appropriate actions and movements and experiment with ways of changing them

Preparation
● Make sure all the children are sitting where they can hear and see you.

What to do
● Introduce new rhymes to the children without the actions, then add the actions, talking through them as you go (eg, 'Here's Incy Wincy climbing up the drainpipe.'). Go through the words and actions slowly, again, encouraging the children to join in and copy.
● Repetition is vital to allow children to develop confidence, skills and imagination. They will want to practise their favourite rhymes over and over again. Whenever you gather the children for a circle time, or have a few minutes to fill, allow them to choose some well-known ones, then introduce one or two new ones, and end with a few favourites.

Extension/variation
● Keep adding to the children's repertoire.

Multicultural link
● Invite parents of English as Another Language (EAL) children to teach a familiar rhyme to the group, using sound and movement.

Links to home
● Invite parents in for an 'Action rhyme session'. This will help parents to learn the same words and actions, so that the children can repeat them often at home.

Topic
Any topic

Resources
■ Rhymes from pages 177 to 182

Weather report

Topic
Weather

Resources
- For words of 'I hear thunder' see page 177
- Paper
- Writing/drawing implements
- Percussion instruments

Learning objectives
- To listen to and join in with a familiar rhyme, anticipating key phrases
- To participate in an action rhyme with the group
- To respond to a discussion of the weather with relevant comments

Preparation
- Teach the children the nursery rhyme (see page 177 for words).

What to do
- Invite the children to stand in a circle to sing the rhyme. Suggest some basic actions to add to the song. These might be:
  - Nothing for the first line
  - A hand behind their ear, then hands open for the second line
  - Fingers wiggling in the air for the 'pitter patter' of the raindrops
  - Stomping their feet for the end of the rhyme.
- Encourage the children to add their own ideas to act out the rhyme while singing it.

- Ask the children to try to think of other words for raining, ie when it is really pouring down (teeming), when it is light but steady (drizzling), or when it is raining on and off (showery). Ask, "Could you fit those words into the rhyme in place of 'pitter patter'?"
- Ask the children to think of words for the thunder. Encourage them to think of loud noise words that describe the thunder: *boom*, *clash*, *bang*, *thump*, for instance.

Extensions/variations
- Be aware of children who are frightened of thunderstorms, and provide extra support and reassurance for them throughout the topic, while encouraging them to try to overcome their fear.
- Draw weather pictures and label them.
- Make a weather book showing different kinds of weather.
- Use percussion instruments to create sounds to go with the song.

Taking turns

Learning objectives
- To learn rhymes by heart and speak them clearly with others
- To take turns to listen and respond, developing an understanding of conversational skills

Preparation
- Introduce the children to the rhymes you are going to use at different times.

What to do
- Tell the children you are, together, going to sing, or say, some rhymes that ask questions and give answers. Suggest that some of the group ask the questions and the others provide the answers.
- Choose the two groups. Help the children to sing or say the rhymes, taking appropriate turns.

Extensions/variations
- Ask the children if they noticed which words rhymed in each rhyme.

Topic
Any topic

Resources
- A set of as many question-asking rhymes as you can think of – eg 'Tommy Thumb'; 'Pussy-cat, Pussy-cat'; 'One, two, three, four, five', etc (see Rhymes, pages 177–182)

- Swap the groups over and help the children to remember whether they are now questioners or responders.

Make a new rhyme

Topic
Any topic

Resources
- A rhyme the children know well, such as 'Twinkle, twinkle little star' (see pages 177–182)
- Flip chart
- Pen

Learning objectives
- To listen attentively and respond to rhymes with relevant ideas and comments
- To recognize rhyme and rhythm in spoken words
- To begin to recognize and read the new words chosen
- To sing songs and speak rhymes and experiment with ways of changing them

Preparation
- Practise reciting or singing a well-known rhyme with the children.

What to do
- Suggest that it would be fun for the group to make up their own rhyme. Begin just by changing the rhyming word – eg 'star' – and encourage the children to think of ways of making the wording appropriate. For instance, they might come up with:

    Twinkle, twinkle, little car
    How I wonder where you are
    Far away where it is night
    With your headlights shining bright etc.

- When they the children can do this confidently, encourage them to begin with new words that don't rhyme with 'star'. Then lose the 'twinkle, twinkle' bit, until you end up with a totally different rhyme, using only the rhythm of the original.
- You will need to work over several sessions to develop the children's ideas this far.

Extensions/variations
- Make posters showing your new rhymes and help the children to 'read' and recite them.
- Make a book of your own new nursery rhymes.
- Choose a rhyme that is relevant to a topic you are exploring in other areas, for instance if you are working on numbers, try to make up different words to 'Two, four, six, eight… .'

All clap hands

Learning objectives
- To join in with repeated refrains and key phrases in songs and rhymes
- To sing songs and speak rhymes and experiment with ways of changing them
- To move confidently in a range of ways, showing good control and safely negotiating space

Preparation
- Teach the rhyme:

    We all clap hands together
    We all clap hands together
    We all clap hands together
    As children like to do.

What to do
- Arrange the children in a circle, standing or sitting in a space. Ask the children to give examples of things they might do instead of clapping hands. Give individual children opportunities to make up a verse of the rhyme. Encourage them to think of things they haven't chosen before – *stamp our feet, stand up, twirl round, shrink down small, reach up tall, roll our hands, tiptoe round, etc.*

Extensions/variations
- Give the children the opportunity to take turns in being leader and deciding what to do next.
- Use the rhyme to practise different forms of movement, direction, etc.

Topic
Any topic

Resources
- Space

Clapping the pattern

Topic
Any topic

Resources
- No special requirements

Learning objectives
- To listen to and reproduce rhythmic sound patterns
- To develop an understanding of syllables

What to do
- Tell the children that you are going to clap somebody's name. They need to listen very carefully to see if they can work out who it is. Clap your own name. Give the children opportunities to decide whose name it is. Repeat the clapping each time someone gets it wrong. Watch the children's faces to see who understands and who does not. Tell them it is your name. Clap it again with them listening. Ask them to clap with you.
- Repeat the process, using a child's name. Repeat again. Ask for a volunteer to clap her own name and encourage the other children to say whether they agree with the clapped pattern, Play this game often, in circle times and spare moments, to allow the children to practise and reinforce their understanding of rhythms.

Extensions/variations
- When most of the children demonstrate a clear understanding of clapping a rhythm, clap a nursery rhyme that they know well, for them to identify.
- Clap a chosen rhyme together.

Related activity
- Copy me (see page 49)

Which came next?

Learning objectives
- To maintain attention and concentration throughout an appropriate activity
- To follow instructions involving several actions
- To explore the different sounds of instruments
- To represent ideas through music

What to do
- Make sure the children are sitting all together, ready to listen and concentrate. Have the instruments laid out in front of them.
- Tell the children that you are going to play a game in which they will take turns to play the instruments. Invite a child to come to the front of the group and make a sound with an instrument, then ask them to sit down again.
- Invite a second child to copy the first sound and then to make another sound, of her choice, with another instrument. A third child can then be invited to make the first and second sounds and to choose and make a third sound. Continue the game in this way.
- The children will have to concentrate hard to keep the activity going. When they have lost track, begin again with different children making different choices.

Extension/variation
- Give a group of children one instrument each and build up a sequential pattern of sounds. Encourage the watching children to direct the orchestra so that it makes the same sequential pattern.

Related activity
- Copy me (see page 49)

Topic
Any topic

Resources
- A range of musical or sound instruments, such as chime bars, bells, tambour, sticks; rain-stick, shakers, triangle, etc

Picture pairs

Topic
Any topic

Resources
- Rhyming pairs template on page 168
- Magazines, cards, catalogues, etc that can be cut up
- Scissors
- Card
- Glue
- Felt-tipped pens

Learning objectives
- To concentrate and maintain attention during a group game
- To understand rhyme through listening to words spoken aloud

Preparation
- Photocopy the template on page 168 on to thin card. It could be coloured in first. Laminate the sheet of card, then cut it into ten small cards as indicated.

What to do
- Spread all of the cards in front of the children. Go through the cards with the children, making sure that they all know what each one shows. Turn the cards face down. The children take turns to turn over a card and say its name, then turn over another one and identify that, too. If the words rhyme, the child takes the pair. The children can be encouraged to count the number of pairs they each have at the end of the game, with support if necessary. If there are any pictures left over the children should decide together which sets they belong to and place them correctly.

Extension/variation
- Ask the children to help you look for more pictures (from magazines, cards, catalogues, etc) which you can add to the game.

Rhyming names

Learning objectives
● To listen closely to the sounds in words and respond appropriately
● To understand the similarities in rhyming words

Preparation
● You need to have introduced the children to the idea of rhyme before you play this game.
● Prior to the activity, look at a list of the children's names and think of words that rhyme. The rhymes don't have to 'make sense' as long as they help children to get the idea of rhyming.

What to do
● The idea of the game is to find, or make up, words which will rhyme with a child's name. If your own name is easy to rhyme, use it as a demonstration – eg, 'My name is Jane and it rhymes with rain', so that children can understand easily. Explore the children's names. If their first name hasn't a word that rhymes with it, perhaps their middle name does, or their last name. If none of the names is easy to rhyme, encourage the children to find as many different beginning sounds as they can, until they find a rhyme that they think is suitable, or funny enough.

Extensions/variations
● At the end of the game, see how many of the rhyming names the children can remember and recite.
● Take opportunities to make 'mistakes' and call the children 'accidentally' by the chosen rhyming name when you are working on other things.

Related activity
● Silly words (see page 105)

Topic
Myself

Resources
■ No special requirements

"My name is Amber and it rhymes with clamber!"

Hey Diddle Diddle

Topic
Animals

Resources
- For words to nursery rhyme see page 182
- Space
- Paper
- Paints
- Paintbrushes

Learning objectives
- To join in with rhyme and alliteration within a group
- To listen to a rhyme, accurately anticipating key events and phrases and responding with relevant actions
- To sing a song, make up movements and experiment with ways of changing them

Preparation
- Teach the children the nursery rhyme (see page 182 for words).

What to do
- Say the nursery rhyme very slowly. Ask the children to curl up in a ball and listen out for when you say 'The cat and the fiddle'. At this point they should uncurl and stretch themselves into cat shapes, and prowl like cats. When you get to 'The cow jumped over the moon', encourage them to leap on all fours to show the cow jumping over the moon. For the dish and the spoon, ask them in pairs to hold each other's hands and dance together on the spot.

- Once the children are confident with the words and the 'storyline', encourage them to develop their own actions and movements as individuals and to work independently to speak and act out the rhyme.

Extension/variation
- Paint pictures of the rhyme and make a display of them.

Little Miss Muffet

Learning objectives

● To show interest in rhyme and alliteration and sing a song within a group
● To listen to a rhyme, accurately anticipating key events and phrases and responding with relevant actions
● To develop control and coordination in large and small movements
● To make up movements and experiment with ways of changing them
● To work with others to create an imaginative sequence and act out a narrative

Topic
Animals

Resources
■ For words to nursery rhyme see page 181
■ Space
■ Drum or tambour

Preparation

● Teach the children the nursery rhyme (see page 181 for words).
● Talk about curds and whey with the children and what they might be. If any of them come from a rural or farming background, they might know that they are the different parts of milk. Ask them to think about what Miss Muffet would probably have been eating and whether they have had anything similar, like porridge, yoghurt or bread and milk.

What to do

● Suggest the children act out the rhyme. Practise each movement first. Begin with them sitting on the floor, cross-legged. Encourage them to make exaggerated scooping and eating movements, to show Miss Muffet eating the curds and whey.
● To practise being spiders, encourage the children to curl up as small as they can, then to open themselves out into spidery shapes and scurry along the floor on hands and feet. They can also practise running away on tiptoes as Miss Muffet, making a suitably scared expression.
● Make a slow, rhythmic beat on the tambour as you say the words, encouraging the children to act out their parts as you recite.
● Once the children are confident with the words and the 'storyline', encourage them to develp their own actions and movements as individuals and to work independently to speak and act out the rhyme.

Extensions/variations

● Notice children who have difficulty in following a percussion beat and offer support if needed.
● Encourage the children to be imaginative and controlled in their movements.
● Suggest that the children take turns to be the spider and Miss Muffet, working in pairs or as two groups to act out the sequence.

**Communication and Language
with Literacy**

Huff, puff

Topic
Animals

Resources
- The story of *The Three Little Pigs* (for storyline see page 185–186)
- Three lightweight pieces of fabric (eg chiffon scarves)
- Space for children to sit and listen, and move

Learning objectives
- To join in with repeated refrains and anticipate key events and phrases in a story
- To respond to parts of a story with relevant actions

Preparation
- Read or tell the story of *The Three Little Pigs* to the children. Emphasize the chorus of 'I'll huff and I'll puff and I'll blow your house down!' Practise huffing and puffing.

What to do
- Group the children into three teams, sitting in lines, one child behind the other. Tell the children that they are going to play the 'Huffing and Puffing' game. The chorus this time is, 'I'll huff and I'll puff and I'll blow your scarf away'.
- The first child in each team stands and holds a scarf. They have to let go of the scarf and huff and puff to see how far they can make it travel. When the scarf drops they sit down at the spot the scarf has reached. The next child in the team takes the scarf and starts from there.
- Continue until all the children are sitting down. To finish the session, ask the children to retell the story.

Extensions/variations
- You can play with balloons but they are harder to control!
- Play with just a small group and let them all have a scarf.
- Encourage children to challenge themselves to move most quickly or travel the furthest with their team.

Act-a-story: Goldilocks

Learning objectives
● To listen to a story, accurately anticipating key events and responding with relevant comments and actions
● To cooperate as a member of a group to develop and act out a narrative

Preparation
● You will need to be familiar with the story of *Goldilocks and the Three Bears*. With the card, draw and cut out three bowls, three chairs and three beds. You could also make some trees to be the wood, and a little cottage.

What to do
● Choose children to hold the cards. Choose someone to be Goldilocks, and three children to be the three bears. With the help of all the children, check that the children who have the parts know what they have to say when you reach the repetitive bits of speech.
● Begin to tell the story. Have the children with the cottage and the wood hold up their pictures for the first part.
● Introduce the three bears with their three bowls. Encourage them to join in. You say, 'The first bear was...' and the child says '...a great big bear'; you say, 'The second bear was...' and the child says '...a middle-sized bear', etc. Encourage the children to use a 'great big' voice, a 'middle-sized' voice and a 'small, wee' voice throughout the story by saying, for example, 'The first bear said in his great big voice... .'

Extensions/variations
● Retell the story as many times as necessary so everyone who wants to can have a turn at being part of the acting out.
● Encourage the children to act out, or improvise, the story without supervision.

Topic
Animals

Resources
■ Story line for *Goldilocks and the Three Bears* (see page 183)
■ Card
■ Scissors
■ Felt-tipped pen

The Three Billy Goats Gruff

Topic
Animals

Resources
■ The story of *The Three Billy Goats Gruff* (see storyline, page 185)

Learning objective
● To listen to a story, accurately anticipating and predicting key events and phrases and responding with relevant comments

Preparation
● If this is the first time you have introduced the story, first read it to the children, showing them the illustrations.

What to do
● Go back to the beginning of the story, telling the children that this time you are all going to tell the story together.
● Begin by making a silly mistake, like saying, 'Once upon a time there were three billy goats gruff all in the shopping centre…' so that the children can correct you.
● Tell the story a little at a time, encouraging the children to fill in key words and phrases by pausing at the right moments. For example, you could say, 'The three billy goats were eating the…?'
● Encourage the children to listen attentively, so that they can anticipate what is should come next and join in.

Extension/variation
● Use the same strategy when reading or reciting rhymes, so that the children can anticipate the rhyming patterns and the rhyming words.

Run, run – The Gingerbread Man

Learning objective
● To listen to stories, accurately anticipating key events and responding with relevant actions

Preparation
● You will need to be familiar with the story of *The Gingerbread Man*.

What to do
● Explain to the children that you are going to tell the story of *The Gingerbread Man* and they are going to be the gingerbread man running away. Ask who can remember the words that he says as he runs.
● Decide on some 'running rules'. For example:
   ◆ Everyone runs in the same direction, without touching anyone else at all.
   ◆ As soon as you say 'And stop' all the gingerbread men stop running and sit down so that you can continue the story. Make sure the children know you will not continue until they are all sitting quietly and ready.
● After the children have run away from everyone else and reached the part where they climb on to the fox's back suggest that they do their climbing on the spot and lie down 'on the fox's back'. When the fox tosses them up into the air, they can jump up and then 'make themselves gone' when they land! At this point they need to be totally still and silent so that you can 'see' that there are no gingerbread men left anywhere!

Topic
Food and shopping

Resources
■ The story *The Gingerbread Man* (see storyline, pages 186-187)
■ Lots of space
■ Paper
■ Writing and drawing implements
■ Ingredients for Gingerbread men:
   125g butter
   60g soft brown sugar
   90g golden syrup
   1 beaten egg
   250g plain flour
   30g self-raising flour
   1 tbsp ground ginger
   1 tsp bicarbonate of soda
   1 tbsp currants
■ access to an oven

Extensions/variations
● Make a display of the repetitive words eg, 'run, run as fast as you can' and 'read' them with the children.
● Invite the children each to draw a picture of themselves as *The Gingerbread Man* and display the pictures with the words.
● Make and bake gingerbread men. Preheat oven to 180°C/350°F/Gas Mark 4. Line 2 baking trays with baking powder. Cream butter, sugar, golden syrup. Add egg slowly, mix. Add dry ingredients. Mix to dough. Roll out. Cut into shape. Add currants for eyes. Bake for 10 minutes.

Be a storyteller

Topic
Any topic

Resources
- Whichever stories or books you wish to tell

Learning objective
- To listen to stories, accurately anticipating key events and phrases and responding with relevant comments, questions and actions

Preparation
- Read the story in a picture book several times, until you have grasped the main characters, events and bits of repetitive language. Rehearse it in your mind before you tell it. Be prepared to adapt and shorten or lengthen the story to suit the children's attention and their enthusiasm to participate. Try to find some 'props' that will help you to tell the story. For instance: puppets or finger puppets; cut-out pictures; any object that acts as a visual aid for you and for the children.

What to do
- *Telling* the story, rather than *reading* it, gives you the opportunity to be spontaneous about where and when you offer it. As you're telling the story, you can watch to see how the children are responding, who is participating and who is not, how enthusiastic they are, and how much attention they are displaying.
- Think ahead about specific actions and intonations that you can use. Leave pauses where the repetitive words and phrases come in, so that the children can anticipate what's coming next. Make it interesting and fun, using all your powers to dramatize and emphasize the rhythm of the story and the words you want the children to pick up.
- Their response will tell you how well you are doing!

Extension/variation
- There's a place for both telling and reading and, don't forget, *making up your own stories*!

Related activity
- Making puppets (see page 54)

Picture stories

Learning objectives
- To listen and respond to others with increasing attention and recall
- To maintain concentration on pictures and answer relevant questions, in order to make up stories

Preparation
- Make a collection of pictures that show a scene with something happening.

What to do
- Discuss the pictures. Ask questions such as:
  - ◆ Who can we see in the picture? If there are people – are they a family? Who do you think each person is? If there are animals – are they *real* animals or perhaps toy animals? What relationship do they have to each other?
  - ◆ Where is the event happening? Is it daytime? Night-time? Early morning? Afternoon? Evening? How do we know?
  - ◆ What things can we see in the picture?
  - ◆ What might be happening?
  - ◆ Are they going somewhere? Have they been somewhere?
  - ◆ What do we think is going to happen next? If this was a story, how would it end?

Extension/variation
- As the children get used to this kind of activity, ask them to try to put their explanations into sentences. Write down the sentences as they are composed, to make a story. At the end, read the story back to the children and ask them if they think they, or you, have missed anything out.

Topic
Any topic

Resources
- Pictures from magazines, catalogues, posters, etc
- Paper
- Writing implements

Swapping stories

Topic
Any topic

Resources
■ No special requirements

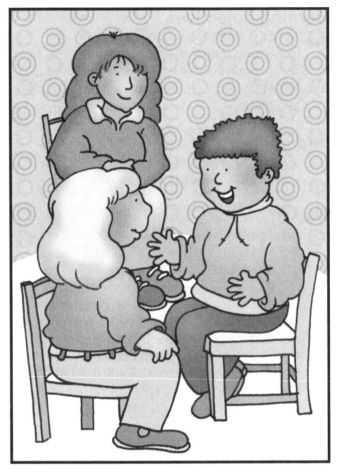

Learning objectives
● To listen attentively to stories with increasing attention and recall
● To focus attention and follow directions
● To follow and retell a story without pictures or props

Preparation
● Read, or make up, a story that you can easily remember; it needs to be one that is not familiar to the children.

What to do
● Explain to the children what is going to happen. First, you will tell a story to one of the children while the other is doing something else.
● Then the first child will tell the story to the second child, with you listening but not interrupting.
● Then the second child will tell the story back to you, with the first child listening but not interrupting.

● When the story has been told for the last time, you will all discuss the stories and decide whether anything was missed out or added, or if anything was in the wrong order, etc.
● Decide which version of the story is the 'best' version and why. Read or tell the original version to compare it.

Extension/variation
● Invite the children to pass on the story to two more children in the same way and then discuss the stories with them all.

Simply a story

Learning objectives
- To listen to stories with increasing attention and recall
- To maintain attention, concentrate and sit quietly during an appropriate activity
- To select and use technology for a particular purpose

What to do
- Choose a simple storyline. You could use or expand one of the ones given on pages 183–187, or make up your own.
- Read out the story to the children. Suggest that you give them each a copy of the story to take home to illustrate and share with their family.
- Sit at the computer, with the children around you. Type in the story as you go through it again, with the children helping you to 'remember' it.
- When you have finished typing, read out the story, asking the children to check if you have made any mistakes.
- Print off a copy for each of the children.
- 'Read' through the story again with the children, then send the stories home for the children to illustrate.

Extensions/variations
- Ask the children to bring the stories back so that you can all look at each other's illustrations.
- Make a display of the stories.

Topic
Any topic

Resources
- Computer
- Word processing program
- Paper
- Printer
- Storylines from pages 183–187

Communication and Language

Understanding

- The greatest tool that children have to allow them to develop skills in language, and in all other areas, is their imagination. Role-play, especially with simple, open-ended resources such as cardboard boxes, encourages children to improvise and think, to listen and respond to ideas expressed by others and to negotiate in conversation and discussion in order to solve problems and achieve desired outcomes.

- Through talking with adults and peers while engaged in imaginative play, children develop an understanding of the words used to describe actions (jump, carry), prepositions (under, behind) and concepts (big, heavy). They begin to respond to sequences of instructions, that may involve several different ideas or actions, to follow stories without pictures or props and to understand questions involving 'who', 'what', 'where, 'how' and 'why'. With the right encouragement, they will answer such questions while describing their own experiences and in response to stories or events.

- Conversation, discussion and role-play offer children opportunities to re-create real-life experiences or to imagine future world fantasies, to pretend to be animals or to act out scenarios as characters from history or favourite stories, communicating both verbally and non-verbally. They can learn new vocabulary and consolidate skills in putting words together confidently to express ideas and to construct more complex sentences. Communicating with others in this way also allows children to participate, to identify with each other's feelings and reactions and to feel empathy. Adults may sensitively help them to re-create and come to terms with less happy experiences, or to practise and prepare for something that is going to happen, such as a group outing.

- All suggestions for imaginative role-play can be used as starting points for engaging children and adults in satisfying communication activities that lead to vocabulary extension and language enrichment.

© Irene Yates
www.brilliantpublications.co.uk

Making jigsaws

Learning objectives
- To follow simple instructions and exchange ideas with others
- To create short sentences in meaningful contexts

Preparation
- Photocopy the Jigsaw template on page 169 onto thin card. Colour in the picture if you wish. Cut along the heavy lines.
- It is easy to make your own puzzles. Choose big, clear pictures from catalogues or magazines. Stick them to card to make them easy to handle. Cut the card into five or six large, irregular pieces.

What to do
- Tell the children you have made a jigsaw puzzle for them, and you can't work out how to put it back together by yourself.
- Look at the pieces of card with them and ask them to tell you everything they can see. Encourage them to describe what they think is happening in the picture. If they run out of ideas, offer a few cues to help them such as, 'Look, there's a baby in a buggy and there's a Mummy with her hands out in front of her. Do you think she could be pushing the buggy?'
- Be ready to help them expand their vocabulary as they discuss the pieces of picture. When they have finally worked out what the picture is about, ask them to try to put it back together.

Topic
Any topic

Resources
- Jigsaw template on page 169
- Old catalogues
- Magazines
- Card
- Scissors
- Glue
- Sticky tape
- Pen
- Hole punch
- String/wool

- Talk about what they can see – were they right?

Extensions/variations
- Use sticky tape on the back to stick the picture back together. Ask the children to make up a few sentences that you could scribe as a caption for it.
- Make several jigsaw pictures with sentence captions, punch holes in them and tie them together to make a book. Encourage the children to share it and 'read' it with each other.

What's under here?

Topic

Any topic

Resources

- Old calendars
- Self-stick notes
- Bits of paper
- Reusable mastic adhesive
- Easel (optional)

Learning objectives

- To respond to instructions and ideas expressed by others in discussion
- To answer how and why questions
- To link sounds to letters and recognize familiar names

Preparation

- Choose an interesting large picture from an old calendar and cover it with either self-stick notes or small pieces of paper stuck on with reusable mastic adhesive.

What to do

- Put the covered picture on a wall or an easel, facing the children, and tell them that you have a 'secret' picture which you are going to uncover a little bit at a time. They are going to have to use their eyes and all their thinking skills to work out what the picture is.
- Take off one self-stick note or piece of paper and ask the children to tell you what they can see. Encourage them to verbalize as much as they can about the small amount of picture they can see – telling you the colours, whether they can see any specific

thing or part of a thing, etc. Ask them to tell you what they think might be under the next piece of paper before you remove it.

- Uncover the picture slowly, stimulating as much speech and vocabulary from the children as possible. When you are almost at the end ask them each to predict what they think the picture might be and why.

Extension/variation

- When the children are familiar with their written names, write them in large 'bubble writing' and cover them up in the same way, asking the children if they can predict whose name is being uncovered from the letters they can see as you remove the pieces of paper, one by one. Say the sounds with the children as you uncover the letters.

Links to home

- Ask parents to donate their used, large calendars to you as these are a good source of clear and attractive pictures and photographs that can fit many topics and themes and be linked to many areas of learning.

Where can Bear go?

Learning objectives

- To respond to simple instructions
- To demonstrate understanding of prepositions by carrying out actions
- To use everyday language to describe positions

What to do

- Take a teddy bear or similar toy and sit with children in a group. Suggest to the children that you could ask them, individually, to put the bear in a special place.
- Choose a child to place the bear, for example, 'on top of something'. The child sits down and you ask the group if she is right. Choose someone else for the next go. Ask the child to place the bear, for example, 'at the side of something'. That child sits down and again you ask the group if she is right. And so on.
- Other positions to ask for are:
  - ◆ In front of
  - ◆ Behind
  - ◆ Underneath
  - ◆ Below
  - ◆ Opposite
  - ◆ Inside
  - ◆ Beside
  - ◆ At the back of
  - ◆ Across from
  - ◆ At the bottom of
  - ◆ At the top of
  - ◆ First, second, last, etc.
- Point out that some of the words or phrases mean the same thing.
- You can develop this game by asking the children if they can put the bear, for example, 'in front' of one thing but 'behind' something else. This will be much more challenging for many of the children.

Extensions/variations

- Invite the children to paint pictures of the bear in its different positions.
- Write a caption for each painting, saying, for example, 'Can you see Bear in front of the books?' or 'Bear is under the chair.'
- Make a display and read all the captions aloud with the children.

Topic
Toys

Resources
- A toy, such as a bear

What does he like?

Topic
Toys

Resources
■ A puppet or toy

Learning objectives
● To follow instructions involving several ideas
● To listen and respond to ideas expressed by others
● To hear and say the initial sounds in words
● To extend vocabulary using initial sounds

Preparation
● Make sure the children all know the name of the puppet or toy.

What to do
● Have the children sitting comfortably together, in a circle. Begin by introducing the puppet. For example: 'This is Ben the Bear. He likes things that begin with the sound of his name. So he likes things that begin with 'b'.' (Avoid saying 'but'.) Ask the children to take turns to think of things that begin with the relevant sound.

● To begin with, the children will think only of nouns – for example, *bubbles*, *bath*, *biscuit*. Lead them to think of things that Ben might like *doing* – ie verbs – as well. For example, *bouncing*, *baking*, *building*. Then think of things that might describe what Ben is *like* – ie adjectives, such as *beautiful*, *bright*, *bumpy*.

Extension/variation
● Play a memory game adding on all the things that Ben likes. For example, if the first person says *bubbles*, the second person could say *bubbles and baths*, and the third person might say *bubbles and baths and biscuits*. Encourage the children to help each other to make the list as long as they can before they get into a muddle.

© Irene Yates
www.brilliantpublications.co.uk

Pass the toy

Learning objectives
- To follow instructions
- To listen and respond to ideas expressed by others

Preparation
- Make sure the children are sitting quietly, in a circle, ready to listen and concentrate.

What to do
- Explain to the children that you are going to pass one of the toys or objects around the circle. The game is that each person has to say something different about the object and they have to listen hard so that they do not say something somebody else has already said.
- Give an example to begin with. If you are holding a doll say, 'This is a doll,' and pass it to the next child, who might say something like, 'It's got curly hair.' And so on.
- When the children have run out of things to say, you could ask, 'Can anybody think of anything different at all?' Help with some gentle clues if you can think of things yourself. If the object has definitely been exhausted, start with another one.

Extensions/variations
- Make the game harder by asking the children to remember and say all the things that were said before their turn, in the right order.
- Instead of a toy, use objects that you use in other areas – for example a musical instrument or a piece of maths equipment.

Related activity
- I went on a bus… (see page 20)

Topic
Toys

Resources
- A small selection of toys and other objects

Class

What can we do?

6–8

Topic
Myself

Resources
■ The words to the song 'Here we go round the mulberry bush, (see page 182)

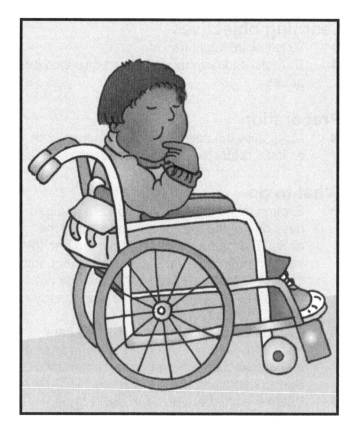

Learning objectives
● To follow instructions involving several ideas or actions
● To learn and remember the names of different parts of the body
● To move confidently with good control and coordination

Preparation
● Teach the children to sing the song. The way the game is played is that the children go round in a circle as they are singing the first two lines. Then they stop, facing inward to do the action. Repeat as often as you wish.

What to do
● You can teach the children the names of actions and of body parts while they are playing this game.
● Give the children lots of different actions, on each occasion that you play the game (but not all at once!). For example:
  ◆ *We wash our faces*
  ◆ *We clean our teeth*
  ◆ *We comb our hair*
  ◆ *We shrug our shoulders*
  ◆ *We wave our hands*

◆ *We fold our arms*
◆ *We stick out our tongues*
◆ *We hang our heads*
◆ *We twist our wrists*
◆ *We wriggle our fingers*
◆ *We pat our knees*
◆ *We point our toes*
◆ *We point our elbows*
◆ *We stand on our heels*
◆ *We raise our eyebrows* .

Extensions/variations
● Use actions like digging, jumping, climbing, tiptoeing, etc, to give the children opportunities to explore whole body movements.
● Use actions like smiling, crying, being angry, so that the children can get used to making different facial expressions.

Copy me

Learning objectives
- To follow instructions involving several ideas or actions
- To listen attentively and maintain concentration
- To imitate simple repeated rhythms and understand how they can be changed

Preparation
- Make sure the children are sitting together, ready to listen and concentrate.

What to do
- Play a clapping game asking children to imitate rhythms. Explain what you want them to do. Clap once and say, 'Copy me.' Clap twice and say, 'Copy me.'
- Ask the children to listen to the number of your claps and count to clap the same number of times themselves.
- Once they can do this, begin to clap simple rhythms, such as two fast claps and one slow clap or one slow clap and three fast claps.
- Invite the children to take turns to clap a rhythm for you and the group to copy.

Extensions/variations
- Clap the children's names and encourage them to practise clapping them with you.
- Play a game where you clap a name and the children have to work out whose name it is.
- Clap specific numbers for the children to count.

Related activity
- Which came next? (see page 29)

Topic
Myself

Resources
- No special requirements

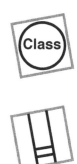

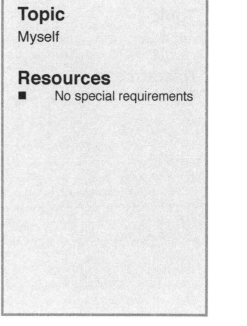

Stand or move

Topic
Any topic

Resources
- A large space

Learning objectives
- To reinforce knowledge and understanding of rhyme
- To follow instructions involving actions
- To develop listening and thinking skills

Preparation
- You need to have done some work on rhyming sounds before this activity.

What to do
- The children need to be in a large space, standing so that they can turn around without touching anyone else.
- Explain that you are going to play a game called 'Stand or Move'. Choose a word together, for example, *cat*. Explain that you are going to call out a word that might or might not rhyme with that word. If the word you call out rhymes then the children must move on their spot. If the word doesn't rhyme they must freeze and stand still. Encourage all kinds of on-the-spot moving and shape-making, but if they move when the word doesn't rhyme they should sit down. If the word does rhyme but they stand still they should also sit down. Call out a series of words until you've exhausted your ideas, or only two or three children are left standing. Praise all the children for their participation, especially those who did not have to sit down, then choose a new word together and invite everyone to stand up and begin the game again.

Extension/variation
- Encourage children to take turns to be the caller and think of rhyming words. You will need to stand close to them and support them in their choices.

Related activity
- Silly words (see page 105)

Build a den

Learning objectives
● To listen and respond to ideas and instructions expressed by others
● To answer 'how' and 'why' questions about experiences
● To use talk to organize, sequence and clarify thinking, ideas, feelings and events and to develop narratives and explanations
● To respect the ideas of others, to work and play cooperatively and to develop positive relationship with peers
● To confidently try new activities, to choose resources independently and to ask for help when it is needed

Preparation
● Find a suitable place in which to make a den, such as a corner area or a space between furniture. It might be helpful to move a piece of furniture closer to one of the walls so that the children can balance the sheet on it to make a roof. If they are building it outside, a garden table or large piece of play equipment might help.

What to do
● Invite the children to build a den in the place you have prepared and suggest that they might like to pretend to be particular characters, such as soldiers, explorers, people on holiday, shipwrecked sailors, pirates or forest rangers, while they work together. Offer materials and resources and encourage the children to design and build their den independently, asking for help or support when they need it.
● When the den is built ask if you may visit it. Encourage them to ask you in and describe the various parts of it and tell you who they are (the role they are playing) and what they are doing there.

Extensions/variations
● Ask the children if there is anything else they need to improve their den.

Topic
Any topic

Resources
■ Fabric such as an old sheet
■ Big piece of furniture (eg table, large piece of play equipment)
■ Cushions
■ Building blocks
■ Throw and/or rug
■ Cardboard boxes
■ Old telephone
■ Resources for picnic (either pretend or real)

● Give the children the opportunity to return to the same play on other days. Den-building can become gradually more sophisticated, as children develop skills and ideas, and they will often return to it to enhance imaginative games or construction play.
● Give the children resources to 'picnic' in the den (either pretend or real).

Hospital area

Topic
People who help us

Resources
- Corrugated cardboard
- Paper
- Card
- Scissors
- Felt-tipped pens
- Cardboard boxes
- Yoghurt pots
- Glue
- Toy medical equipment, if available
- Stapler
- Pencils
- Bulldog clips
- Cushions
- Safety pins
- Towels, fabric, etc

Learning objectives
- To use language to imagine and recreate roles and experiences
- To answer questions about experiences and events and respond to ideas expressed by others during discussions
- To link statements to a theme and use past, present and future forms accurately when talking about events
- To play cooperatively with others and to represent thoughts and feelings through role-play

Preparation
- Talk to the children about their experiences of hospitals, eliciting as much vocabulary from them as possible.

What to do
- Suggest to the children that you set up your own hospital corner, where they, or the toys, can be patients. Invite as many ideas from them as they can come up with.
- Use corrugated cardboard to make screens, cardboard boxes with the tops cut off to make beds for the toys. Use dolls' pram and cot mattresses, pillows and blankets for the beds. A pillow, a blanket, or even a piece of cardboard, can provide a stretcher or a trolley for a sick toy.
- If the children are going to be patients, lay towels on the floor to be beds, and fold another towel or tea-towel at the bottom of the 'bed' to be a blanket.
- Make upside down watches out of card and attach them to the uniforms to be worn by the nurses and doctors. Cut medicine bottles and spoons out of card.
- Make patients' records with A4 paper attached with a bulldog clip to a piece of card, and put one at the bottom of each bed, with a pencil. Help the nurses and doctors to fill the charts in and write notes on each record and to write out 'prescriptions'.
- Make a cardboard box 'chair' (box with the top and one side cut out) for the side of each bed and provide a list of times that visitors may come into the ward. Make yoghurt pot flower pots for each patient.
- Make a clock for the wall and delegate one of the nurses to ring a bell or tell the visitors when they must leave.

Extensions/variations
- Make a little book of hospital words.
- Give the children lots of opportunities to talk about their real hospital experiences.
- Give opportunities for recounting imagined experiences.
- Make get-well cards for the patients.

Be a pirate

Learning objectives
- To extend children's vocabulary and answer 'how' and 'why' questions in response to stories and events
- To use language to imagine and recreate roles, experiences and storylines in play situations

Preparation
- Make a pirate ship out of a big cardboard box, cover a section of floor space with paper or a sheet to be a treasure island.

What to do
- Discuss with the children the meaning of 'pirate'.
- Show the children the pirate items you have made and collected. Ask the children to describe them, name them and tell you what the pirate would need them for.
- Talk about the kinds of hazards pirates might face, such as storms at sea, sharks, huge waves or other pirates who might want to take their treasure.
- Set off a small group of children at a time to be pirates in their pirate boat, sailing to the island to look for treasure.

Extensions/variations
- Have a plenary session where different groups of 'pirates' tell the others how they got on.
- Make up a pirate song.
- Give opportunities for discussing the experiences.

Related activities
- Message in a bottle (see page 157)
- Treasure map (see page 156)

Topic
Water

Resources
- Large cardboard box
- Paints
- Paintbrushes
- Large sheets of paper or sheet
- T-shirt
- Eye-patch
- Earring
- Painted cut-out parrot
- Treasure map
- Scarf
- 'Gold' coin
- Jolly Roger flag

Making puppets

Topic
Any topic

Resources
- A favourite storybook
- Paper bags
- Coloured felt-tip pens
- Bits of fabric and coloured paper
- Glue
- Elastic bands
- Wool or string
- Cardboard box
- Paper plates
- Paper
- Glue

Learning objectives
- To answer questions about characters and events in stories
- To use a variety of language to recreate stories
- To construct with a purpose in mind, using a variety or resources, tools and techniques

Preparation
- Share one of the children's favourite stories with them.

What to do
- Talk about the characters in the story. Show the children the illustrations and discuss what the characters look like. Ask the children who their favourite character is and why. Encourage them to talk about the other characters and say who they like or don't like and why. Ask what each character does, whether they are good or bad characters and how the children can tell.

- Suggest that the children make puppets of the characters, so that they can dramatize the story.
- Paper bag puppets are easily made. Invite the children to draw and colour their chosen character on to the bag. Provide pieces of fabric or coloured paper for them to stick on to make their characters even better.
- When the puppets are ready, the paper bag is slipped over the hand and secured around the wrist with an elastic band or piece of wool.
- The children are now all set to re-enact the story with their puppets.

Extensions/variations
- Make a little puppet theatre out of a cardboard box.
- Make puppets with paper plate faces and rolls of paper stuck to the back of them like sticks.
- Ask the children to retell the story to you before they go off to try it out together.

Sew-sew

Learning objectives
- To show understanding of prepositions by carrying out actions
- To respond to and follow simple instructions
- To handle materials and tools with increasing control

Preparation
- Cut the card into shapes appropriate to other key areas or topics you are working on. For instance, if you are working on a topic involving shapes, cut out geometrical shapes; if you are investigating animals, cut out simple animal shapes.
- Use the hole punch to punch a pattern of holes around the edges.

What to do
- Give each child a card shape and let them choose some coloured wool. Show them how to thread the wool in and out through the punched holes. Use appropriate vocabulary all the time – *in and out, through, back, front, over* – to reinforce the children's understanding of the words.
- This activity will help children to develop the pincer grip, between first two fingers and thumb, that they will need to hold a pencil effectively for drawing and writing.

Extensions/variations
- Help the children to cut our their own shapes from card and to choose where to make the holes.
- Thread several different colours of wool through the holes to make more complex patterns.

Topic
Any topic

Resources
- Strong card
- Scissors
- Hole punch
- Coloured wool

Wordless books

Topic
Any topic

Resources
- Card
- Scissors
- Colouring pens
- Ring clips
- Hole punch

Learning objectives
- To follow instructions involving several ideas
- To answer questions and offer thoughts about experiences and stories
- To use talk to organize, sequence and clarify ideas, feelings and events
- To use art to represent ideas, thoughts and feelings as a story

Preparation
- A book does not have to have *words* to make it work. Make up a book with a series of pictures and no text.

What to do
- Explain to the children that your book has pictures but no words. The pictures tell the story. Explain that you are not going to write the words of the story because everybody is going to be able to look at the pictures and remember it.
- Encourage the children to work out what the story should be, then invite them to make coloured pictures of the events and stick them to pages. When all the pictures are ready, carefully order them with the children and then join them together in the correct sequence. Invite the children to create a cover design together.

- Encourage the children to look through the book and retell the story together.

Extensions/variations
- Look for wordless picture books in the local library. The most famous one is probably *The Snowman* by Raymond Briggs. Many modern reading schemes begin with wordless books, to introduce their characters.
- Encourage the children to read the pictures and tell the story to other children, adults, visitors and their parents.
- Make up stories by using a series of photographs linked to other themes or topics you are exploring in the group – eg, you could show, in sequence, pictures of the children cooking or making something.

Related activity
- Right order (see page 72)

© Irene Yates
www.brilliantpublications.co.uk

Make one like it

Learning objectives
- To create and follow a new story without pictures or props
- To recognize and understand rhyme and alliteration
- To begin to read words and simple sentences

Preparation
- Choose a strongly patterned storybook, such as *Brown Bear, Brown Bear, What Do You See?*

What to do
- Read the book to the children, several times. Encourage them to join in with the choruses and leave gaps for them to fill in.
- Suggest to the children that you all make up your own story, just like the Brown Bear one, using the same pattern, but different ideas.
- Invite suggestions for changing Brown Bear into something else. Point out the alliteration and encourage them to use the same concept – for instance, *Cool Cat*, *Magic Mouse*, *Fat Flea*.
- Carry on making up the story with the children to fit the pattern. The funnier it is, the better. Write their words down as you go along, and read them back with the children.
- When they decide the story is complete, write it on to pages, put it together to make a book and invite the children to illustrate it.

Extensions/variations
- Read the children's new story back with them.
- Encourage the children to learn and chant the words of the new story as you point to them.
- Leave the original book and the children's book in an accessible place for sharing and for comparison.

Links to home
- Invite children to take turns to take the book home to share with their family

Topic
Any topic

Resources
- A strongly patterned storybook, such as *Brown Bear, Brown Bear, What Do You See?* By Bill Martin and Eric Carle (Picture Lions)
- Flip chart
- Felt-tipped pen
- Card
- Paper
- Treasury tags
- Hole punch

Talking about stories

Topic
Any topic

Resources
- A selection of known storybooks
- Paper
- Drawing implements

Learning objectives
- To develop an understanding of the different elements of stories
- To answer 'how' and 'why' questions about their feelings and opinions in response to stories

What to do
- Read the story to the children, encouraging them to join in if they can and if the story is familiar.
- Afterwards, discuss the story by asking the children questions, such as:
    - Who, or what, is the story about?
    - How did the story begin?
    - How does the story make you feel?
    - Does it make you feel happy? Or sad?
    - Why?
    - Which character do you like best in the story?
    - Why?
    - Which character do you like least in the story?
    - Why?
    - Which is your favourite part of the story?
    - Why?
    - How does the story end?
    - Is it a good ending?
    - Why?
    - What do you think of this story?

Extension/variation
- Ask the children to draw something – an event or a character – from the story and think of a sentence or two for an adult to scribe, or to write, copy or trace with support.

Acting stories

Learning objectives
- To follow and remember a story without pictures
- To speak within a familiar group and to respond to ideas expressed by others
- To confidently try new activities, to choose resources independently, to attempt problem solving and to ask for help when it is needed
- To play cooperatively within a group to develop and act out a story and to represent ideas through role-play

Preparation
- Choose a story the children know well. Recap the main events of the story with the children.

What to do
- After discussing the story, offer props and costume items to the children and suggest that they might choose their own roles and act out the story.
- Become an observer while they plan and negotiate, but offer support with problem solving where necessary. (For instance, if they are acting out 'The Three Billy Goats Gruff' they may want to build something that represents a bridge. Their ideas may lead them to put chairs together – not a good idea! Guide them to see that the bridge can be imagined from laying something flat on the floor.)
- Only intervene when absolutely necessary: the children will hit obstacles in their re-enactments but will develop their problem-solving and thinking skills by overcoming them.

Extension/variation
- Sometimes re-enactments turn into 'favourite games' for a while. If this happens, encourage the children to swap roles and see/act the story from every perspective.

Related activity
- The Three Billy Goats Gruff (see page 36)

Topic
Any topic

Resources
- A bank of well-known children's stories (see Storylines, pages 183–187)
- Appropriate costume items and props

How would I feel?

Topic
Myself

Resources
- Paper plates
- Drawing implements
- Puppets

Learning objectives
- To follow a story without pictures or props
- To listen and respond to ideas expressed by others
- To answer questions about experiences and in response to stories
- To speak confidently to others about own feelings and opinions
- To talk about how people show feelings

Preparation
- You will need to think of some scenarios prior to the session (see below).
- Have the children sitting together, ready to listen and concentrate.

What to do
- Tell the children that you are going to tell them some little stories and you would like to see what they think of them.
- Give them various little scenarios that you would like them to respond to. For example, say, 'Just imagine – it's the weekend and you have asked your best friend to come and play at your house. You've been waiting and waiting for her to come. You've thought of all the games you can play together, and got all your toys out. Then, just before she's supposed to arrive, her mummy phones and says they can't come! Make a face that *shows* me how you would feel. Now stand up and *show* me how you feel.'
- After the children have all acted out their feelings, ask them to sit down again and stop pretending to feel cross or sad. Invite children to volunteer to tell the group how they felt.
- Repeat the activity using different scenarios – getting an unexpected present, going somewhere you never thought you would be able to go, somebody you love coming when you didn't expect it, etc – and encourage the children to put their feelings into words that match their expressions.

Extensions/variations
- Use paper plates to make expressive faces.
- Use puppets to act through the scenarios, with the children verbalizing the puppets' thoughts and feelings.

Communication and Language

Speaking

- It is hard for children to communicate effectively when they are not sure of their language ability. Sometimes they find it hard to express themselves clearly when speaking to other children and to adults. Undivided attention and warm responses from adults will help the child to develop feelings of self-confidence and satisfaction. Interaction with adults and peers enable children to develop the ability to communicate and become aware of the different needs of their listeners.

- Children can speak if someone listens to them. Adults can encourage language development, and the ability to talk to organize, sequence and clarify thinking and ideas, by being responsive, waiting, listening carefully and offering praise to reinforce correct speech. It is also important to be aware of body language and to understand the clues that children give while expressing their needs and feelings. Adults must avoid talking for children, helping them when they don't need help, interrupting or steering conversations, or assuming that they already know what the children want to say.

- All children develop gradually, at their own speeds, in their own ways, and adults need to remain aware of this, remembering to accept their abilities at the present time, as well as encouraging further progress. Offering unlimited opportunities for conversation, along with games and activities involving speech, will enable children to learn to use past, present and future forms accurately, to increase their vocabulary and to develop their own narratives and explanations as they connect ideas and events.

Observe, wait and listen

Topic

Any topic

Resources

■ No special requirements

Learning objectives

● To take opportunities to speak
● To verbalize ideas and express them effectively
● To use talk to organize, sequence and clarify thinking

Preparation

● Use this strategy during all play and learning situations.

What to do

● Remind yourself of the three important key words – Observe, Wait and Listen – when the children are in any speaking situation:

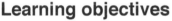

  ◆ **Observe** the child's focus of attention, facial expression and body language – this will help you to understand what the child is speaking about.
  ◆ **Wait** for the child to communicate first. Not always easy, but try not to control the moment by taking over.
  ◆ **Listen** attentively to what the child says – let the child do most of the talking; if you feel he/she needs prompting, do it gently.

Extensions/variations

● Give positive feedback to speakers all the time.
● Help children to interpret ideas and feelings when they get stuck.
● Encourage all children to express their own feelings, needs, wishes, opinions and interests.

Multicultural links

● Be sensitive to gaps in vocabulary with children for whom English is an additional language.

Links to home

● Ensure that you are a good role model for parents by observing this approach with their children and explaining its benefits.

© Irene Yates
www.brilliantpublications.co.uk

Speak and listen

Learning objectives
● To extend vocabulary and explore the meanings and sounds of new words
● To link statements and connect ideas

What to do
● Three important concepts for helping children to develop language skills are:
  ◆ Imitate
  ◆ Interpret
  ◆ Comment
● When you imitate what the child says, she will know you are listening to her. For example, if she says 'Oh no!' and you say, 'Oh no!' as well, you interpret and you confirm that you have received the child's message. If you add, 'What's happened here?', for example, you have shown that you have guessed what the child is trying to put into words and can help her to say it. She might say, 'It's all felled down,' and you can say, 'It's all fallen down?' Repeating what the child says, with a question in your tone, will encourage the child to try again.
● Explaining that you don't understand and asking her to try again, will confirm your interest in what she has to say.
● When you comment upon what the child is doing, you are helping her to learn new vocabulary.

Extension/variation
● Look for opportunities during all activities to reinforce vocabulary and language structure.

Multicultural links
● Be sensitive to gaps in vocabulary and language structure with children for whom English is an additional language. Just comment clearly and naturally, so that the children absorb your language patterns.

Links to home
● Demonstrate these techniques clearly while parents are present so that they may imitate and use them with their children.

Topic
Any topic

Resources
■ No special requirements

What is it?

Topic
Any topic

Resources
- Toys and other small play equipment
- Feely bag (a bag to put objects in; the objects need to be heard and felt, but not seen)

Learning objectives
- To use descriptive vocabulary to clarify ideas and develop explanations
- To express concepts effectively, showing awareness of listeners' needs

What to do
- Tell the children that you are going to play a game that is all about *describing* things. Explain that 'describing' means telling what something is like. For instance, they might describe one of the children. Ask for a volunteer who doesn't mind being 'described' and help the children to verbalize descriptive phrases or sentences about that child.
- Suggest to the children that you play a game and invite the child who volunteered to go first. Ask everyone else to turn around and sit with their backs to the child. Give the child a toy or piece of equipment. The child now has to describe the object in simple phrases, giving every clue she can about what she can *see*. Help the child to talk about shape, size, colour, texture and the material it is made from.
- Challenge the other children to guess what the object is. Invite the first person to guess correctly to take a turn at describing another object.

Extension/variation
- Make a feely bag. Let the children touch objects inside it and describe what they can feel.

Communication and Language with Literacy

Tell us about ...

Learning objectives
- To speak clearly and audibly about chosen objects or events, showing an awareness of listeners' needs
- To speak confidently within a familiar group and communicate ideas freely

Preparation
- Ask the children to take turns to bring something from home that they would like to show to the rest of the group. Write out a list detailing when each child's turn will be, taking into account the days and sessions that they attend, if not all full-time. Make the list available to parents and explain the purpose of the activity, allowing at least a few days notice of each child's turn.

What to do
- Create a regular occasion when children from the group 'show and tell' to the rest of the children. Make simple rules, such as:
    - All children sit still, quietly and attentively to be a good audience.
    - Everyone has a turn to bring something in to the group.
    - Everyone learns to listen.
- Group the children in a way that is not threatening to the speaker, and be ready to encourage and prompt if necessary. Try not to intervene if the child who is speaking doesn't need your help. Allow her to choose her own words and verbalize her own ideas and thoughts to describe what she is showing the group.
- Work towards a situation where the group can organize and run their own 'Tell us about…' sessions independently of you, so that you are merely an observer!

Extensions/variations
- Having something to hold and show makes it easier for the child to speak in front of the group but also encourages children to talk about less concrete things, such as things they have done and events in their lives. Encourage them to bring in something small

Topic
Any topic

Resources
- No special requirements

and symbolic as an opportunity to talk about times that were significant or important to them, such as being a bridesmaid, going to a wedding, having an operation or visiting the dentist, etc.
- Encourage the children to talk to the group about activities and tasks they have completed or enjoyed at the setting.

**Communication and Language
with Literacy**

Make and play

Topic
Any topic

Resources
- Paper plates
- Sticky tape
- Card
- Scraps of fabric
- Wool
- Glitter
- Buttons
- Felt-tipped pens
- Elastic bands
- Scissors
- Coloured papers
- Glue sticks

Learning objectives
- To use talk to organize and sequence thinking and ideas
- To introduce a storyline or narrative into play
- To play cooperatively within a group to develop and act out a narrative

Preparation
- Have all the materials easily accessible so that the children can see what is there and make independent choices.

What to do
- Invite the children to make their own puppets and use them in creating a play. Discuss what their play might be about and who their puppets might be. Help them to decide on characters.
- Each child needs a paper plate for the head of the puppet. Invite them to draw, cut and stick to make the face and the hair.
- Roll pieces of card lengthwise to make 'sticks' to fix to the back of the puppets. Help the children to choose fabric to make the puppet's clothing and fix it to the stick, which will form the puppet's neck, with an elastic band.
- The children then hold their puppet by the stick, under its clothing, and make it perform.

Extensions/variations
- Suggest that each small group works out a little play and performs it to the rest of the group.
- Encourage the children to talk to each other, and to you, through the puppets at all opportunities.

Links to home
- Invite the parents in to see the puppet shows.

Fish and chips

Speaking

Learning objectives
- To use intonation, rhythm and phrasing to make meaning clear
- To listen attentively and respond to what is heard
- To sing songs and experiment with ways of changing them

Preparation
- Teach the children the French song 'Frère Jacques' so that they are familiar with the tune.

What to do
- Explain to the children that you are going to make up your own song, fitting the words to the tune that they know. Stick to something simple, like food, to make it easy for them.
- Beat out the rhythm of the first line with sticks, four beats, and ask the children to think of words for a line that will fit.
- Do the same with the other lines.
- You should come up with a song such as:
  Fishy fingers, fishy fingers,
  Chips as well, chips as well,
  Sausage and spaghetti, sausage and spaghetti,
  Beans on toast, beans on toast.
- The children will enjoy singing their song to visitors and will be enthused to make up more.

Extension/variation
- Do this with other simple well-known tunes, such as 'Twinkle twinkle, little star', 'Three blind mice' and 'Seesaw, Margery Daw'.

Topic
Food and shopping

Resources
- No special requirements

Collecting

Topic
Gardening/environment

Resources
- Plastic bag
- Card
- Pencils
- Paper
- Crayons
- Felt-tip pens

 Ensure correct child : adult ratio if leaving the setting.

Learning objectives
- To extend vocabulary and descriptive skills to reflect experiences
- To explore the meanings and sounds of new words
- To talk about objects from nature, to draw them and write labels and captions

Preparation
- Make sure the children are dressed suitably for going outside.

What to do
- Tell the children you are going on a 'nature walk' to make a collection of natural objects which you can then display in your room. Either take them outside to explore the garden or outdoor area, or take them for a walk to a local park, wood or green.
- Encourage the children to observe and talk about what they can see around them.
- Collect interesting seasonal objects – for example, conkers, acorns and blackberries in autumn, common wild flowers in summer. When you get back to your setting invite the children to draw the things they saw and collected. Write captions with them. Ask them to decide on the words, then help them by writing the words for them to copy or trace over. Make a display of the items and the children's work.

Extension/variation
- Make a list of all the new words the children have encountered. Read the words with them and invite individual children to make an illustration for each one. Add to the display.

Links to home
- Ask in advance for volunteer parent helpers to accompany staff and children on their walk.

What's outside?

Learning objectives
- To use past, present and future forms accurately when talking about events
- To develop narratives and explanations by connecting ideas
- To talk and ask questions about the natural world and the local environment
- To develop an understanding of patterns and change
- To talk about the seasons

Preparation
- Make sure the children are dressed for the weather and for the location.

What to do
- Take the children outside and talk with them about how it looks and feels. Ask questions, such as: Is it cold? Is it warm? Is it very sunny? Is the sky blue or is it cloudy? Has it been raining? How can you tell? Does anyone know what the season is called? Give the children the names of the four seasons and remind them which season you are in currently.
- Ask them if they can remember the previous season. Help them by asking questions, such as: What was the temperature like? What was the weather like? What did the trees look like? Were there lots of flowers or no flowers? What were the bushes like? Talk about the types of clothes that they wore and what they might have worn on their feet.
- Ask the children which season they think will come next and what it might be like, what they might wear and whether they might do anything special (eg, celebrate Christmas in the winter or go on holiday in the summer).
- Encourage the children to think deeply about the changing pattern of the seasons. They may not yet be old enough to have become very aware of them, especially now that the temperatures and weather conditions in Britain have become so much more random and extreme. Offer them as much new vocabulary as possible.

Topic
Seasons

Resources
- An outdoor exploration area
- Paper and writing/ drawing implements

Extensions/variations
- Make a 'Seasons' book showing all the changes the children can think of.
- Play a game in which one person names a season and the rest of the group think of different things to say about it.

Making stories

Topic
Any topic

Resources
- Approximately five objects, such as a toy, a birthday card, a picture, an item of clothing, a piece of fruit
- Paper
- Writing and drawing implements

Learning objectives
- To create a narrative or storyline by connecting objects and ideas
- To work cooperatively within a group to develop a narrative or storyline and to make up an imaginative story

Preparation
- Make a collection of objects – you could collect these by asking various children to choose something to bring for the story. The children need to be sitting quietly, as for circle time.

What to do
- Explain to the children that you are going to make up a story together. Show the children the collection of objects you have made. The idea is to make up a story that has as many of the things in it as possible. The story also has to make as much sense as possible.
- Before you start, ask, 'Who will our story be about?' You might find that the children want to stick to known characters to begin with, until they have the idea, but that's fine; they can be more adventurous later!
- Go round the circle asking each child to make a contribution to the story. Keep the objects on view so that the children can remember what they are, and they will act as a stimulant to the development of the story.

Extension/variation
- If the children are excited by the story they have made up, invite some of them to help you to put it into a book, by making the illustrations and telling you which words to write with them.

Order, order

Learning objectives
- To use talk to organize and sequence ideas and events
- To retell a story by connecting events in order

Preparation
- Photocopy the Order, order template (page 170) on to thin card. Colour it in if you wish. Cut the sheet up into separate cards. Laminating the cards will make them last longer.

What to do
- Mix up the cards of each set. (Don't mix the sets together!)
- Look at the cards with the children, asking them what they can see. Suggest that if the cards were in the right order they would 'tell a story'.
- Ask the children to put them into the right order and 'read' the story to you.

Extensions/variations
- For children with advanced sequencing skills, cut out stop strips from comics and ask them to work in pairs to put the story into the right order and then 'read' it to you
- Make up your own sequencing cards.

Related activity
- Right order (see page 72)

Topic
Any topic

Resources
- Order, order template on page 170
- Thin card
- Felt-tipped pens
- Scissors
- Laminator (optional)

Right order

Topic
Any topic

Resources
- Paper or card
- Felt-tipped pens

Learning objectives
- To use talk to organize and sequence ideas and events
- To retell a narrative by connecting ideas and events in order

Preparation
- Using a storybook that the children have shared with you, draw and colour simple pictures of the main events, one to each piece of card, and mix them up. If you are not a confident artist, you could photocopy selected pictures and stick them onto pieces of card.

What to do
- Tell the children that you have made some pictures of the story they liked but now that you've finished them you need some help to put them in the right order.
- Put all the pictures down on a flat surface, in any order, and ask the children to look at them and tell you what they can see. If you don't tell them what the story is, you will give them the added interest of trying to 'guess'.

- Encourage the children to look at each picture and describe in words what they think is happening in it. Let them do as much of the talking as possible, between them, offering support only when they struggle to find the words they need or run out of ideas.
- Their next task is to lay the pictures in the order in which the story happened – encourage them to use time and sequencing words and phrases, such as 'in the beginning', 'at the start', 'to begin with', 'and then', 'next', 'last of all', 'this is how it ended'.
- When the pictures are in the right order, encourage the children to use them to retell the story aloud.

Extensions/variations
- Use stories with a repetitive refrain. When the children decide that the refrain needs to be in the sequence, write the words for them on more pieces of card and invite the children to place them in the correct places between the pictures.
- Help them to 'read' the words.

Related activity
- Order, order (see page 71)

Make musical instruments

Learning objectives
- To use talk to connect ideas, explain what is happening and anticipate what might happen
- To use talk in pretending that sounds stand for something else in play
- To link statements and stick to a main theme or intention
- To use talk to organize, sequence and clarify thinking and ideas
- To use and explore a variety of materials and techniques, experimenting with design and function

What to do
- Tell the children that you are going to make a range of special musical instruments together. Show them all the items you have collected and ask them if they can think of any ideas. Treat the process as a problem-solving activity, inviting children to give their ideas and experiment to see if they work.
- Make different sounds:
    - Clap yoghurt pots together, or tap sticks together.
    - Put seeds or pebbles into one yoghurt pot. Tape a second yoghurt pot firmly to it and use as a shaker.
    - Use containers of different sizes and materials as drums.
    - Fix string or elastic bands across blocks of wood and pluck them.
    - Fill bottles and jars with different levels of water and tap with pencils or dowels.
    - Stick sandpaper to two wooden blocks and rub them together.
    - Hang eight different lengths of wood from a stick with string and pull a dowel across them.
    - Tie milk bottle tops to a dowel and shake them.
    - Tap pieces of wood and metal together.

Extensions/variations
- Encourage the children to describe different sounds to you.
- Ask them if they can make quiet sounds and then loud sounds.

Topic
Any topic

Resources
- Yoghurt pots
- Sticks or dowels
- Seeds
- Pebbles
- Sticky tape
- Bottles and jars
- Water
- Milk bottle tops
- String
- Elastic bands
- Containers
- Sandpaper
- Blocks
- Glue
- Small wooden strips
- Metal objects

- Ask them to make light sounds and then heavy sounds.
- Discuss which sounds they would use for a mouse, a monster or an elephant.

Dressing-up box

Topic
Any topic

Resources
■ Large cardboard box
■ Clothing items
■ Shoes
■ Jewellery
■ Mug holder
■ Hats

Learning objectives
● To use language to imagine and recreate roles and experiences
● To develop a storyline or narrative by connecting ideas and to introduce it into play situations
● To interact with others, exploring and negotiating plans and playing cooperatively within a group

Preparation
● Make sure the dressing-up box is always easily available. Hang the jewellery on the mug holder.

What to do
● Encourage the children to sort through the dressing-up box to find items they want to wear and to choose the activity independently, whenever they wish to during free play times.

● Give lots of positive feedback – ask the children when they are dressed up, 'Oh, who has come to visit us this morning? Where have you been? Where are you going?' and encourage them to have conversations with adults and peers in role, when they are happy to do so. But respect the value of the children's own imaginative ideas and do not intervene too much or try to change or steer or take over leadership of the games.

Extension/variation
● Dressing-up games are often continuous – a child enjoys dressing-up games and playing a particular role for a certain length of time, until they have satisfied the need to explore it fully and express their feelings, and then moves onto a new role or a different type of play. Allow this to happen naturally.

Links to home
● Invite parents to donate any unwanted outfits, clothes and accessories to the dressing-up box.

Space shuttle

Learning objectives
- To use language to imagine and recreate roles, experiences and storylines in play situations
- To extend vocabulary, link statements and stick to a theme
- To attempt to write letters, words and sentences to communicate meaning
- To count backwards in ones
- To explore technological equipment and suggest a variety of uses

Preparation
- Talk to the children about journeys into space and check their knowledge about space travel, rockets, shuttles, the moon, stars, planets, etc.

What to do
- Suggest to the children that you make your own space shuttle, so that they can be astronauts and travel through space. Show the children all the materials you have gathered to make the space shuttle and discuss how you can build it together, making it a problem-solving exercise. Use large sheets of corrugated cardboard against a wall as the sides, with a space cut out or folded to make an entry/exit, or docking chamber, and drape fabric or netting across the top. Roll up a piece of card and make a pointed end on it for a rocket or launcher. Cover it with tin foil to give a metallic look, and secure it to the side of the shuttle.
- Inside the shuttle you need perhaps a bedchamber, a desk and chair, and any items of old technological equipment that you can gather from staff, families and local suppliers. Leave writing equipment and 'radio'-phones in the shuttle for constant use.

Topic
Transport and travel

Resources
- Large sheets of corrugated card
- Fabric
- Tin foil
- Netting
- Old phones
- Old fax machines or computers
- Table
- Chair
- Writing materials
- Paints, brushes, etc

- Encourage the children to use 'space' language, and to practise counting backwards for 'lift-off'. When the shuttle is completed, leave them to play.

Extensions/variations
- Make a list of space words that the children know and read them with them.
- Encourage the children to send messages, verbally, in writing and in code, from space to earth.
- Make stars, a moon, and planets and stick them around the space shuttle.
- Make a 'Journey Into Space' book together.
- Give the children opportunities to address the group, talking about their experiences.

Office centre

Topic
People who help us

Resources
- Computers
- Printers
- Telephones (static and mobile)
- Fax machines
- Tables
- Chairs
- Message pads
- Paper
- Pencils
- Pens
- Rubber stamps

Learning objectives
- To extend vocabulary by learning the names of unfamiliar pieces of equipment
- To use language to imagine and recreate roles and experiences in play situations
- To understand uses of objects and follow instructions involving several actions
- To recognize that a range of technology is used in places such as offices and businesses

Preparation
- Collect together as many defunct pieces of equipment as you can, or that you have room for.

What to do
- Set up an 'office centre' as simply as you can. It doesn't need to be complicated at all – just place all the pieces of equipment you have on the tables and tell the children that this is the 'office centre'. Help them to decide what kind of office it is today – doctor's, hairdresser's, business, bank, etc.

- Show the children the message pads and pencils and discuss what they are for.
- Join in the role-play, gently to begin with, helping them to identify all the pieces of equipment and know what they are pretending to do with them. Give the children plenty of time to develop their own games on their own.

Extension/variation
- If you haven't got much space, put the office centre away at the end of the day, and bring it out at different times, rather than all the time.

Links to home
- Ask parents if they have any defunct materials which you could use for your 'office'.

What I liked was...

Learning objective
● To demonstrate an understanding of the main elements and structures of stories
● To speak confidently within a familiar group about experiences, interests and opinions

Preparation
● Read your book and have some ideas about what you would like to say about it.

What to do
● Look at the book with the children and discuss the features that they can see – the title, the author, the illustrations, etc. If there is a blurb on the back, read it out to them. Tell them that you have read and enjoyed the book and tell them about the main characters, the main events, how it began and how it ended. Tell them why you liked it – perhaps it had a good repeating pattern, or it was funny, or it reminded you of something in your life.
● Tell the children that you would like them to tell the group about a book that they have enjoyed, in the way that you have told them – talking about the characters and the main things that happen. Ask them to choose a book and tell the group something about it.
● Record the children's reviews onto the cassette tape and play them back to them.

Extension/variation
● Invite the children to dictate their ideas to an adult. Write them down, invite the children to illustrate them, and make a 'Book Review' display.

Topic
Any topic

Resources
■ A storybook you know
■ Tape recorder
■ Blank cassette tape
■ Paper and writing implements (to make own book)

Re-jig a familiar story

Topic
Any topic

Resources
■ A very familiar story, such as *Goldilocks and the Three Bears* – try to link books with topics you are working on at the time (see storyline, pages 183–187)
■ Paper and writing implements to make own book

Learning objectives
● To explore ideas and express them effectively, showing awareness of listeners' needs
● To develop a new narrative based on a familiar story
● To answer questions in response to stories

Preparation
● You need the children to be sitting in a space where they can listen and talk.

What to do
● Tell the children that you had thought of reading the story of Goldilocks again, but that you are tired of it and wondering whether it would be possible to change it.
● The obvious things to change are:
   ◆ The characters – ie Goldilocks and the bears – Ask the children to decide on their own characters. Maybe they will say something like –'a brave boy and three aliens'.
   ◆ The setting – ie the wood and the little house. Ask the children to make suggestions again. Maybe they will say something like –'a seaside beach and a cave'.
● You could also change the repetitive lines as the children wish, and possibly the outcome, but be guided by the children in this – much will depend upon their level of understanding.

Extensions/variations
● Encourage the children to make a book of their new story.
● Discuss which story the children like best, the original or their new one, and why.

Related activity
● Simply a story (see page 41)

Building stories

Learning objectives
● To understand the elements of stories, such as characters, settings, openings and endings
● To use talk to explore, organize and sequence ideas
● To develop a storyline by connecting ideas and events, using past, present and future forms accurately

Preparation
● Make sure that the children have plenty of experience of listening to stories.

What to do
● Sit in a circle with the children. Explain that the object you have in your hand is specially chosen as a–'story-telling ball/car/bear' today. It will help you all to make up a story. You will start, then you will pass the object around the circle. Whoever is holding the object makes up the next bit of the story.
● It is simplest to begin with what you are holding so say, for example, 'Once upon a time, there was a ball. It was…' Describe the ball and give it a situation, for example, 'The ball was bored. It wanted to do something really different. So it took itself off, rolling along the ground'. Then pass the object on to the first child.
● Help the child to make up another bit of the story. Where might the ball have gone to? For example, '*It went all the way to the seaside, over the hills, and rolling down the lanes, until it got to the sea...*' Help the child to stop at a place somewhere in the story where the next child can easily pick it up. For example, '*and along came a gull who said… .*'

Topic
Any topic

Resources
■ An object to pass round, this could be anything – a ball, car or bear

● If the children get involved in discussion, allow them to use all their problem-solving skills to continue the story – remind them that *anything* can happen in stories! Make sure that the story has an end.

Extensions/variations
● Encourage and support individual children as the retell the whole story to a different group of children.
● Make pictures of the story and write key words beside them. Invite children to tell you which words they recognize.

Who shall I be?

Topic
People who help us

Resources
- CD Player
- Music
- Paper
- Writing implements

Learning objectives
- To develop narratives and explanations by connecting ideas and expressing them effectively
- To use language to imagine and recreate roles and experiences
- To show interest in and knowledge of different occupations and ways of life
- To represent people, experiences and ideas through role-play

What to do
- Invite the children to play a game involving pretending to be other people.
- First of all, everybody sits in a space and thinks of somebody they might be (eg firefighter, window-cleaner, car driver). When everyone is sure they have a person, you start the music. While the music is playing, the children act out doing whatever their chosen person might do. When the music stops they all freeze in position, still pretending to be the person.
- One child is chosen to act out their person first. Everybody else sits down to watch and try to guess who it is. Support the child as she offers verbal clues, descriptions and explanations to accompany her acting, until somebody guesses correctly.

- Begin the music again and ask all of the children to act while it plays. When the music stops, choose another child to speak and perform to the group. Continue until all of the children have had a turn to speak if they wish to.

Extensions/variations
- Help the children decide on role models by suggesting a number of tasks that might be performed by various people.
- Add a 'writing' element to the activity by inviting the children to draw a picture of their chosen person and compose a caption for you to scribe.

Literacy

Reading

- Many children do not have access to books at home and rarely see anyone reading. Practitioners can motivate children to want to learn to read, simply by being good role models and showing that reading is a natural and enjoyable activity.

- Children live in a world that is often confusing and unpredictable, so books can offer them the security of experiencing the same characters, objects, actions and events over and over again. They may believe that the experiences in books are real, or understand that stories are invented, but the clarity and repetition is comforting.

- Talking about books with adults and listening to stories leads children to explore conversational skills, vocabulary, concepts and ideas. They may begin to join in with repeated phrases and to anticipate key events, to describe characters, settings and plots and to become aware of the story structures and endings.

- We live in a literate society and written symbols are everywhere. Children in the Foundation Stage, should be inspired with the confidence that they will learn to read and write when they are ready. Adults need to provide opportunities for children to understand symbols and to know that print carries meaning, to gradually learn and practise the recognition and identification of letters and sounds and to begin to read names, labels, words and simple sentences.

- Children enjoy playing with sounds in games, such as 'I-Spy', or in rhyming or nonsense stories and poems. They can be encouraged and supported as they link sounds and letters, develop phonic knowledge and remember some common irregular words in order to begin to read independently. If an adult reads with children, tracing sentences from left to right with a finger, the children will often recognize the initial sound of a word, think about the context and predict

---

what the word might be. Prediction skills are essential for learning to read. As children's language skills develop, they become more able to predict which word might come next. They should also demonstrate an understanding of what they read, through talking with others, and know that they can find information from books, computers and other sources.

● Matching games can take children quickly from matching pairs of pictures to matching sounds, letters and words. These skills, together with understanding the direction of the print and the gaps between words, will help children to learn to read. Games are an enjoyable way of offering children the experience they need, alongside a more formal framework.

Early years settings don't need lots of expensive commercially produced material because, with a little time and thought, practitioners can make their own games and activities especially for their own group of children.

● Reading books with adults offers children a comfortable feeling of shared imagination, the challenge of new language patterns, new information to absorb, the anticipation of possible danger or new worlds explored safely through stories. Some stories are favourite for along time because they satisfy children's feelings and allow them to identify with characters or events of importance in their own lives. Children who enjoy books will be intrinsically motivated to learn to read for themselves.

Build a castle

Learning objectives
● To know and understand that information can be retrieved from books and computers and from other sources, such as talking to people or watching television
● To read simple words and sentences and to demonstrate an understanding of what is read
● To answer 'how' and 'why' questions about experiences and stories
● To select materials and to use and explore tools and techniques to shape, assemble and join them

Preparation
● Look at some reference books with the children about castles, knights in armour, jousts, etc.
● Ask the children to tell you about any experiences they have had of visiting castles, ruined or otherwise, and to tell you what they know of castles from television programmes, films, DVDs or computer games they may have seen.

What to do
● Suggest to the children that you could build your very own medieval castle. Use corrugated cardboard to make walls against one of the setting's walls. Cut the top of the castle walls to make crenellated parapets or ramparts.
● Make a drawbridge by joining one end of a large piece of card to a space in the castle walls. Tie string to the other end and punch holes at this end and in the two walls. Put string through the holes and use it to pull the drawbridge up and down. Make a moat with an old blue curtain or sheet. Make turrets by rolling up corrugated cardboard and cutting the tops into an appropriate shape.
● Make crowns and cover them with tin foil. Make hats by rolling thin card into a pointed

Topic
Homes

Resources
■ Reference books about castles
■ Corrugated cardboard
■ Paper
■ Card
■ Scissors
■ Felt-tip pens
■ Cardboard boxes
■ Hole punch
■ String
■ Blue curtain/sheet
■ Tin foil
■ Fabric
■ Lots of space

shape and taping a piece of fine fabric to hang down from the point. Make breastplate armour with pieces of card, cover with foil and punch a hole in each of the four corners. Thread string through and secure across the child's back.
● Make a display of books about castles which are accessible to the children and encourage them to share the books with each other and other adults. Give the children as much explanation and information about castles as they can absorb and set them off to play and pretend.

Extensions/variations
● Make a 'This is our Castle' book, with pictures and words for the different parts of the castle.
● Give the children opportunities to address the group, telling how they built the castle and what they have done in it.

Post delivery person

Topic
People who help us

Resources
- Post box
- Lots of letters and cards written by the children
- Post delivery person's costume, items/ accessories
- Bag

Learning objectives
- To link sounds to letters and use initial sounds to read names
- To use phonic knowledge to decode regular words and names and read them aloud
- To remember some common irregular words and names

Preparation
- You need to have made the post box and posted several letters or cards in it.

What to do
- Invite two or three children up to be post delivery people. Find appropriate costume items or accessories, or help them to make some. Provide bags for the children to put the letters and cards into.
- Help the children to open the post box and take the letters out of it. Decide who will deliver whose post.

- Help the children to sort the post, using cues such as familiar names and the beginning sounds of names. Also draw their attention to common irregular words sometimes seen on letters, such as 'to' and 'from'.
- The children should put the letters they are delivering into their bags and set off to deliver them.

Extensions/variations
- Try to give everyone a turn at becoming a post delivery person.
- Use a cardboard box as a postal van and deliver 'parcels'.

Related activities
- Send a letter (see page 163)
- Write me a letter (see page 162)

Same and different

Learning objective
- To observe small differences and similarities between pictures, in preparation for matching and recognizing letters and words

Preparation
- One of the most important skills for reading development is to recognize things that are the same and things that are different.
- Photocopy the Same and different template on page 171. Cut out the cards. Laminate them to prolong their use.
- You could photocopy or use the computer copy facility to reproduce an image to make your own 'Same and different' cards.

What to do
- Talk about the sets of cards. Ask the children to look for *what's the same* and *what's different*. Encourage them to verbalize and describe the differences and similarities.
- Play games with the cards:
  - Put all the cards face up on the table and ask the child/children to collect all the cards which match each other.
  - Put all the cards face up on the table and ask the child/children to collect all the cards which don't match any others.
  - Put all the cards face down on the table and turn them over in turns, trying to make matching pairs.
  - Put all the cards face down on the table and turn them over in turns, discarding the matches and trying to 'catch' all the ones that don't match any others.

Extension/variation
- Make cards with letters or familiar words for very able children and play the same games.

Topic
Any topic

Resources
- Same and different template on page 171
- Laminator (optional)
- Paper
- Card
- Felt-tipped pens
- Scissors

Setting up a book area

Topic
Any topic

Resources
- Table
- Shelves
- Boxes
- Cushions
- Card
- Felt-tipped pens
- Library card

- Choose as large a range of books as possible – make sure that there are picture story books, wordless books, information books, magazines and comics.
- You will probably be able to get a number of books from your local library on long-term loan – and often you can get the librarian to come in and talk to the children about books.
- Explain to the children that all of the books are there for them to share and look at during sessions and you are always happy to see someone 'reading' books, especially if they are reading together.
- At this stage, don't make too much fuss about the books being kept 'tidy' because what you want to do is encourage the children to feel they can handle them freely and look at them whenever they want to.
- Make your display of books look pretty and inviting – you may be able to beg or borrow posters from a local bookshop to enhance your own array of books.
- Make notices to give information or encouragement, such as, 'The Book Area is open today' or 'Come and look for a book with your friend'. Read the notices with the children so that they become familiar with them and know what they say.

Learning objectives
- To understand that books can be meaningful and enjoyable parts of everyday life
- To know that information can be retrieved from books and computers and the knowledge applied to other activities

What to do
- Have a look in your local library and see how the books are made accessible to the children. Usually books for young children are kept at low levels, in boxes with chairs nearby so that the children can easily browse and choose.
- Much will depend upon the space that you have available but aim for a cosy corner where the books can be displayed and the children can sit comfortably to share them with each other and the adults in the setting.

Extensions/variations
- Invite parents to spend time in the book area with some children.
- Have a loan system of your own so that the children can choose books to take home.

Related activity
- Library visit (see page 97)

Communication and Language with Literacy

Be a reading role model

Learning objectives
- To understand that reading is a normal and useful part of people's everyday lives
- To know that print always carries meaning and to explore a range of different reading materials

What to do
- It is important to remember that books are not the only reading material you need to offer to the children. You should strive to provide a good reading environment in which children feel comfortable with all kinds of reading matter.
- Start a collection of all kinds of different material. You can get freebies from lots of different places – shops, stations, information centres – and all of the material will help to make the children aware that reading is not just something that happens in books.
- Use the material, for them to see, whenever you can. For example, if you are going to watch a TV programme, let them help you to look up the programme in the TV guide; if you are making a visit, show them how to locate your destination on a map. You are not aiming at this time to get your children to 'read', but merely to observe how useful reading is in your daily life.
- Make as much use of notes and lists as you can and encourage the children to help you to plan events and outings, using information packs to help you.

Extension/variation
- Make regular trips to the library or the library bus and help the children to understand how the books are sorted.

Links to home
- Ask parents to encourage children to bring leaflets and maps to 'show and tell' when they have been on family trips or events.

Topic
Any topic

Resources
- Brochures
- Maps
- Timetables
- Directories
- Recipe cards
- Magazines
- Comics
- Labels
- Notices, etc

Related activity
- Sharing books (see page 93)

Choosing books

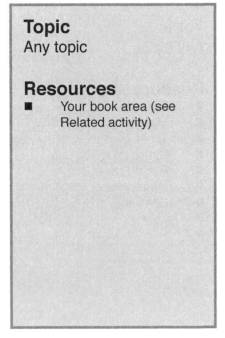

Topic
Any topic

Resources
■ Your book area (see Related activity)

of development – therefore you will need every kind of book from board books with no text or simple one-word-per-page texts, to books with complex pictures and lots of text.

● Look for books that:
   ◆ raise the children's self-esteem by giving them characters with whom they can identify
   ◆ give opportunities for interaction – eg flap books, pop-up books or books asking questions
   ◆ show real people in a real world
   ◆ reflect the children's interests and experiences
   ◆ show people of all races and cultures and people with disabilities
   ◆ tell about characters who have the same kind of worries and problems as the children.

● Add to these, of course, home-made books that you have made with the children in the group or that they have made at home and brought in.

Learning objectives
● To develop an interest in, and enjoyment of, an increasing range of books
● To maintain attention and concentrate on both stories and non-fiction books

Preparation
● Work out how you are going to display your books and make them accessible to the children.

What to do
● It is important that you choose the books you are going to offer the children with great care. You should be looking for a wide selection that will suit all the children's levels

Extension/variation
● Ask the children to take good care of the books and draw up a set of simple rules together for sharing books.

Links to home
● Ask the parents if the children have any favourite books that they would like to share with the group on a lending basis.

Related activity
● Setting up a book area (see page 86)

Looking at books together

Learning objective
- To develop new interests and find increasing enjoyment in a range of books

Preparation
- Try to show the children that you, yourself, enjoy browsing and looking at books, and that books are important to you.

What to do
- Have a looking-at-books session where all the books are out and the idea is to browse. Tell the children that you are all going to spend some time looking at the books, to see what you can see.
- Give them encouragement to choose whichever books they want to look at and give them a comfortable place to sit with their book, or books, and just look at them.
- Some children will find it impossible to browse and choose if they are not used to books at home. Give them as much positive help as you can – say, 'I know a book you would really love – it has great pictures in!', and locate a book that you know will have some interest for that child. Reference books about animals and forms of transport are usually a hit with the boys, who are not always quite so story-orientated as girls.
- At the end of the session, invite individuals to come to the front of the group and talk about their choices.

Extensions/variations
- Encourage children to take books home to share with their parents.
- Encourage children to take turns to choose a book for you to read to the group

Topic
Any topic

Resources
- A broad range of books – board books; pop-up books; storybooks; reference books; picture books, .
- Comfortable furnishing, eg floor cushions
- Paper
- Drawing implements

- Invite the children to make illustrations for their favourite books and to think of captions to write for themselves or for you to scribe for them.

Multicultural links
- Obtain some books that are multicultural in illustration and content.
- Ask parents to lend some books in different languages and alphabets, or purchase dual language books, so that children may see that books come in all languages.

Links to home
- Encourage parents to make sharing books with their children an important part of family life.

Which book?

2–3

All levels

Topic
Any topic

Resources
■ Your book area (see Related activity)

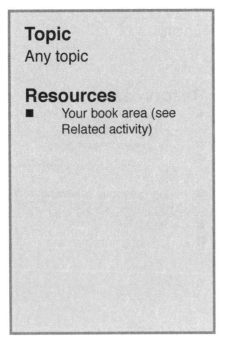

'recognize' the book, ask further questions such as whether they recognized the picture on the cover or the pictures inside, the letters or shape or colour of the title, a character or setting or event. Discuss whether there are more books about the same characters.

Learning objectives
● To demonstrate interest in illustrations and print in books
● To recognize and match familiar types of book, themes, words, pictures and characters
● To use vocabulary and forms of speech that are increasingly influenced by experiences of books

Preparation
● Keep a short time aside for choosing books to look at.

What to do
● Invite children to take turns to choose and find a book that they would like the group to share with them.
● Ask them how they know which book they are looking for. If they tell you that they

Extensions/variations
● Put groups of books together which have a central character, theme or sequence of events and encourage the children to verbalize the differences between them. For example 'This one is about Kipper making a cake, and this one is about Kipper going camping.'
● Bring in new books and ask the children if they can tell what they are about from the illustrations.

Related activity
● Setting up a book area (see page 86)

Time to read

Learning objective
- To begin to read words, using knowledge of letter sounds and phonics and previous experience

Preparation
- Make sure a good selection of books and other material is available and easily accessible to the child.

What to do
- Encourage the child to go through the reading material in order to select something to read with you.
- Choose a peaceful time and a comfortable spot, and be ready to give the reading child your full attention.
- Give the child as much time as she wants to look at the words and the pictures and to respond to them. Encourage her to hold the reading material and turn the pages herself. Wait until it becomes clear that she wants you to read aloud to her.
- Pause for her to fill in the words where she is able and respond by adding in language and reinforcing her knowledge.

Extensions/variations
- Take turns. Give the child plenty of time to say the word or the first part of the word, if she knows it.
- Hold back and reinforce by repeating, when she has got a word right.

Topic
Any topic

Resources
- A collection of all kinds of reading material – books, comics, brochures, etc

Reading together

Topic
Any topic

Resources
■ All kinds of books and print material

Learning objectives
● To enjoy an increasing range of books
● To know that print carries meaning and, in English, is read from left to right and from top to bottom
● To read some common regular and irregular words and to use phonic knowledge to decode others
● To use pictures as clues to anticipate text and to aid understanding

Preparation
● Have lots of books and print material to hand.

What to do
● Encourage the child to choose a book for you to read together. If it is a story that the child is unfamiliar with, read it to her first. Then suggest, 'Shall we read it together?'

● Have the child/children close so that you are giving the activity a feeling of cosiness. Let the child do as much as possible to interpret the pictures and the words, support as necessary and offer hints and prompts as appropriate
● Work together through the text; point with your finger to match the words to the spoken language.

Extension/variation
● Encourage the child to choose a book completely new to her, look through it together first, helping her to anticipate what it might be about, then read it to her.

Sharing books

Learning objectives

- To enjoy books, both independently and with others
- To begin to read words and simple sentences
- To demonstrate understanding when talking with others about what has been read
- To listen attentively to stories, accurately anticipating key events and responding with relevant comments

Preparation

- Make 'sharing a story' a very important and enjoyable time. If you can do this at a specific time on most days (as well as spontaneously at other times), the children will come to anticipate it with pleasure.

What to do

- Good reading habits that last a lifetime come from making children's first introduction to books and stories as enjoyable as possible. Early reading skills are absorbed when we:
  - Make sure the child can see both the print and the pictures
  - Point to the words as we read them, showing the left to right direction
  - Use the pictures, which may have a second 'story' in them
  - Pause occasionally – ask, 'What do you think is going to happen next?'
  - Leave space for discussion where appropriate, before turning the page
  - Encourage the children to 'read' or retell the story to us
  - Go back time and time again to favourite stories.
- Let the children choose the books that they want you to share and ask them, 'What is it about?' 'What do you like about it?' 'Who is the character?' 'What does the character do?' 'Is it a good ending?' 'Why?' etc.
- Encourage the children to join in with the words, or take over the reading from you, whenever they can.

Topic
Any topic

Resources
- Lots of books and other print materials

Extension/variation

- Demonstrate to parents how to share books enjoyably with children, and encourage them to imitate your role at home.

Read it with feeling

Topic
Any topic

Resources
■ A collection of books, both fiction and non-fiction

Learning objectives
● To enjoy an increasing range of books
● To demonstrate understanding of what is read
● To accurately anticipate key events in stories and respond to what is heard

Preparation
● Have your book collection available at all times, where the children can access it easily.

What to do
● Use any occasion that arises to stimulate the children's interest in looking for a book that fits that occasion. You need to know your collection of books fairly well, so that you can immediately say, 'Oh, there's a book about this on the shelf!', and get the children to locate it for you.
● It is much more fun for the children if you read dramatically, emphasizing particular words, or the rhymes or the rhythms that

you want the children to respond to. You can pause before you turn a page, encouraging the children to anticipate the next word, or the next action, or picture – all this will bring the text alive for the children and help them to enjoy it more. If you use dramatic techniques, with varied facial expressions, actions and body language, while reading aloud to the children, you will encourage them to respond and make the experience more enjoyable for everyone.

Extensions/variations
● Changing the name of a character to fit a child in the group or someone known to the group.
● Changing the text a little so that it fits the circumstances you are in.
● Staying with a page that is particularly enjoyable, concentrating on the language, the details in the pictures and asking the children for their ideas about what is on the page.
● Skipping pages that are less interesting.
● If the text is beyond the children's level, telling it in your own words.

Understanding stories

Learning objectives
- To be aware of the way stories are structured
- To retell a story, using vocabulary and forms of speech that are influenced by experiences of books
- To write words and simple sentences, with support, and read them to others

What to do
- Read, or tell, the story.
- Ask the children to draw you a picture of how the story begins, what happens in the middle and how the story ends.
- Ask the children to put their pictures into the right order and 'read' the story to you in storybook language, from their pictures.

Extensions/variations
- Invite the children to dictate the story and to attempt to write their chosen words and sentences beside the pictures. Offer appropriate support to each individual child scribing or providing opportunities for tracing, copying or independent phonetic spelling. Help the children to put the story into the right order, then stick the three pages together with sticky tape to make a zigzag story book.
- Encourage the children to read the story back to you and to share it with other children and adults.

Links to home
- Encourage parents to help their children to make pictures of home events. Ask the children to bring the pictures to the setting and use them in this activity.

Book know-how

Topic
Any topic

Resources
- A broad range of books

Learning objectives
- To understand the structure of books and where to find different pages and sections
- To use and understand book vocabulary, develop prediction skills and begin to read words and simple sentences

What to do
- Every time you pick up a book to look at with the children, use book vocabulary, so that the children absorb it naturally. Talk about 'the cover', 'the pages', 'the illustrations'.
- Try and engender in them a love of books, which is easily done if you are yourself enthusiastic about books.
- Share your reading with them – talking about 'words', 'sentences' and 'letters' and encouraging them to predict what might happen next, what the next word might be, etc.
- Ask them to show you things such as:
  the first page
  the last page
  the top of the page
  the bottom of the page
  the front of the book
  the back of the book
  the beginning of the story
  a word
  a line
  a caption – the words under the picture
  the word that comes next
  the page numbers
  the title
  the author's name.

Extension/variation
- Turn the 'showing' around – show *them* the top of the page, etc, and ask them what it is.

Multicultural links
- Ask parents to lend some books in different languages and alphabet, or purchase dual language books, and demonstrate to children that not all writing reads in the same direction and not all alphabets look the same.

Related activity
- Book words (see page 119)

Library visit

Learning objectives
- To enjoy an increasing range of books
- To raise awareness of library provision in the locality

Preparation
- Try to arrange a pre-visit with the librarian to find out what is on offer. Librarians are only too happy to get children hooked on books right from the beginning and will often suggest running a story time, lending extra books, making a regular visit to the group, etc. It would be particularly helpful if each child could choose a book to borrow.
- You can either take the group as a whole, or do several trips with smaller groups.

What to do
- Discuss the impending visit with the children so that they know what is expected of them. Make the visit as much fun as possible.
- Afterwards, allow the children to discuss the trip on their own terms. Make time to share the borrowed books and talk about them.
- Invite the children to talk about their chosen book to the rest of the group.

Extension/variation
- Arrange follow-up trips.

Topic
Any topic

Resources
- Local library or library van

⚠ Ensure correct adult : child ratio for visit.

Links to home
- Ask for parent helpers for the visit.
- Encourage parents to visit the library with the children and to take out a library ticket for them.

Reading moments

Topic
Any topic

Resources
■ Lots of books of all kinds and other reading material (magazines, comics, brochures, etc)

Learning objective
● To actively seek out books and develop skills in independent reading, for information, imagination and pleasure

Preparation
● Make sure there are lots of books accessible at all times.

What to do
● Children sometimes get the impression that books and reading are only for specific times and places – ie story telling time at the group! Unless they are surrounded by reading material at home and have a reading family, the activity does not appear to them to be a natural one!

● Introduce Reading Moments to them. Any moment can be a Reading Moment. When you have finished one activity and aren't quite ready to go on to another one, why not settle down for five minutes with a book?

● Reading Moments can happen inside or outside, they can be short moments or long moments, they can be sharing moments or solitary moments, they can be profound thinking moments or having-a-laugh moments. Try to get this concept across to the children by demonstrating that you, too, have Reading Moments, and that you enjoy them very much.

● Give lots of positive feedback.

Extensions/variations
● You may have to have one or two simple rules – for example, if someone has a Reading Moment outside, they remember to replace the book carefully in its outdoor storage box or shelf to protect it from messy activities and weather.

● Try to keep Reading Moments as informal as possible. If the children want to talk about what they have read, encourage them, but don't discuss their reading as a matter of course because it will seem to them as though every Reading Moment is followed by a Big Interrogation Moment!

Links to home
● Explain the Reading Moments concept to parents and encourage them to have reading matter available to follow the strategy at home.

Related activity
● Sharing books (see page 93)

Sharing a book

Learning objectives
- To know that print carries meaning and, in English, is read from left to right and from top to bottom
- To read and understand simple sentences
- To accurately anticipate and respond to key events in stories

Preparation
- Choose a book with a repetitive pattern, such as *Brown Bear, Brown Bear, What Do You See?* Read the book to the children and show them the pictures.

What to do
- At the top of each page of your paper, print a part of the story. Read it with the children, tracking each word as you go, and encouraging them to join in.
- Offer each child a small piece of paper to illustrate a part of the story. Stick their pictures to the appropriate pages, making sure that it is the children who decide which of the pages each illustration belongs to. It doesn't matter how many versions of an illustration you stick to each of your large pages as long as the children all contribute to as many as they can.
- Put card at the front and back of your pages, punch holes and use the rings to hold it together.
- Read through the book together, tracking the words. Read the original book with the children again and invite them to make comparisons.

Extensions/variations
- Do this with any of the children's favourites.
- Put the group books in the book corner with 'real' books.
- Invite the children to read and share the books whenever they have a 'Reading moment'.

Links to home
- Encourage the children to take the books home to share with their families.

Topic
Any topic

Resources
- *Brown Bear, Brown Bear, What Do You See?* By Bill Martin and Eric Carle (Picture Lions) or alternative books with strong repetitive pattern
- Sheets of paper 30cm x 45cm
- Black felt-tipped pen
- Smaller pieces of paper
- Glue
- 2 pieces of card 30cm x 45cm
- Hole punch
- Binder rings

Related activity
- Reading moments (see page 98)

Whole words

Any

All levels

Topic
Any topic

Resources
- Card
- Felt-tipped pens

Learning objectives
- To show interest in print in the environment
- To recognize familiar words and signs, such as names, labels and advertising logos

Preparation
- Talk to the children about the words that we see around us every day and encourage them to be observant and to spot both new and familiar words.

What to do
- Discuss the words that you see close to your setting, or in your setting. For example the words 'Push', 'Pull', 'Exit', 'Fire Door' may be around you on the walls and doors.
- Children are also used to seeing their own names and their friends' names in the setting. Encourage them to observe the words – they will soon begin to note, or absorb, the shape and the pattern that the

print makes for each word. Encourage them to remember and recognize the words – this is the beginning of reading.
- Make a collection of the words the children recall seeing, perhaps in the street or the park.

Extensions/variations
- Make a display of the words and draw attention to them when appropriate.
- Link reading and literacy skills with activities in other areas of learning, by looking for numbers in the street, signs at the park and notices in local shops, etc.

Look for words

Learning objective
- To recognize or decode and read familiar words and phrases

Preparation
- Look for spaces and situations that you can easily write words, captions and labels for.

What to do
- Make one of the points of your caption-and label-writing that the children see you do it, read it with you, and understand why it is there.
- For instance, you may want to ask the children to keep the books tidy. Discuss this in circle time, and suggest to the children that you write a label together to remind them. Ask them to help you to decide what the label should say. When you have come to an agreement, demonstrate writing it, read it through together, pointing to the words as you read, and decide together where the label should be placed.
- When you are by the books ask the children to tell you what the label says. Encourage them to point out some of the words. For example, you may ask, 'Which word says 'book'?' and reinforce the beginning sound and letter to help them.

Extensions/variations
- Help the children to write labels and captions for their play situations, eg in the post office write 'Stamps' and 'Queue here', or other phrases that the children want, and regularly ask them to read the words back to you.
- Write familiar words for other areas that you are exploring, draw the children's attention to them and 'read' them together frequently.

Topic
Any topic

Resources
- Card
- Felt-tipped pens

Sound box

Topic

Any topic

Resources
- Large cardboard box
- Card for labels
- Felt-tipped pens
- Magazines (for pictures)
- Scissors
- Glue

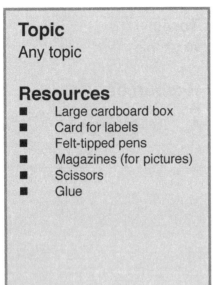

Learning objective
- To link sounds to letters and to hear and say the initial sounds in words

Preparation
- Make a set of labels of initial sounds that you want the children to learn. For each letter sound, cut and stick, or draw, a picture of something the children will recognize. For example for 'b' cut and stick a picture of a bear, as a cue.

What to do
- Have the children sitting in a circle and show them the box. Identify the picture and the sound that you are choosing to use first. Have a short session of thinking of things or words that begin with that sound.
- The game is for the children to take turns to look around the room and locate something that begins with the sound. They fetch the object and show it to the group, who agree or disagree. If the group agrees, the object goes into the box.

- At the end of the game, take out the items one by one, identifying them and their initial sound, and return them to their original location around the room.

Extensions/variations
- Have three sound boxes available at the same time and either invite the children to choose which sound they will try for or ask them to find one for each box.
- Invite the children to bring in things from home for the collections, on specific days.

© Irene Yates
www.brilliantpublications.co.uk

Letter train

Learning objectives

● To link sounds to letters, naming and sounding the letters of the alphabet
● To begin to absorb and remember the order of the alphabet
● To play cooperatively within a pair or small group, taking turns, showing sensitivity to others' needs and forming positive relationships

Preparation

● Enlarge the Letter train template on page 172 to A3 size. Photocopy onto thin card. Colour in if you wish. Laminating will make the game board last longer.
● Children need to be at a steady table or in an isolated place on the floor.

What to do

● Give each child a counter and explain how to play the game. They take turns to move the die and move their counter the number of coaches that they throw, saying the sound that they land on. If they can't say the sound the others must tell them and they repeat it. The game can end either when the first child lands on 'z' or when the last one does.

Extensions/variations

● More able children could be asked to give up to three words beginning, or ending, with the sound they land on.
● Make another board with capital letters, and support children as they play the game in the same way.
● Ask the children to play the game with either board, saying the letter names rather than their sounds.

Topic

Transport and travel

Resources

■ Letter train template on page 172
■ Felt-tipped pens
■ Laminator (optional)
■ Die
■ Counters

Reading

Guess what it is

Topic
Any topic

Resources
- No special requirements

Learning objectives
- To hear and say the initial and ending sounds in words
- To listen and respond to ideas expressed by others

Preparation
- Have the children sitting together ready to listen and concentrate.

What to do
- Tell the children you are going to play a game called 'Guess what it is'. Look around the room and focus on an object, but don't give them too much of a visual clue to begin with because their eyes will follow yours and you want them to think about listening, not looking.
- Suppose, you had chosen 'book'. Say, 'There's something I can see that begins with the sound 'b' and ends with 'k'. Can you guess what it is?' (Make sure you do not add 'uh' to the sounds.)
- When the children have had lots of practice at the game, invite them to take turns to choose an object for others to guess.

Extension/variation
- Instead of finding things in the room, think of things that the children might know and give an extra clue, for example: 'I'm thinking of something that begins with 'sh' and ends with 'p' and lives in a field.'

 Communication and Language with Literacy

Silly words

Learning objectives
● To identify and understand rhyming sounds within spoken words
● To think of and match rhyming words and to explore and experiment with sounds within words

Preparation
● Have the children sitting together ready to listen and concentrate.

What to do
● Tell the children you are going to play a game called 'Silly words'. You are going to say a word and they are going to tell you as many words as they can think of that *sound* the same *at the end*. Give an example, such as *blow* and *grow*. Examine the sounds of the words with the children, ask which bit sounds the same and which bit sounds different. Give another word that rhymes, such as *toe*. Again, check the understanding of which bit sounds the same and which bit sounds different.
● Ask the children to give you as many more words as they can think of, ending with the sound of 'oe' (as in *toe*). When they have run out of 'real' words, encourage them to make up 'silly' words.

Extensions/variations
● Explain to the children that when words sound the same at the end, we say that they *rhyme*, and we call them *rhyming* words.
● Ask the children for other examples of rhyming words that they know.
● Play this game with different sounds, many, many times.
● Make the game appropriate to activities you are working on in other key areas by choosing words about what you are doing, for instance if you are cooking you might begin with *bake* and *cake*.

Related activity
● Rhyming names (see page 31)

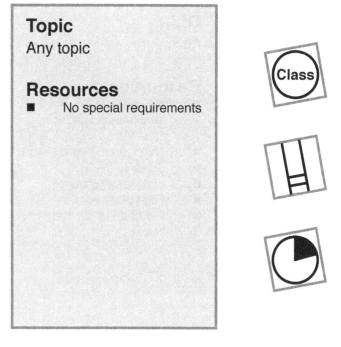

Topic
Any topic

Resources
■ No special requirements

Some rhyming, one-syllable sounds to use are:

ai	grey, pray
er	fir, fur
air	chair, hair
ee	bee, tea
ear	here, fear
ie	by, dry
ake	cake, bake
or	four, door
oa	toe, grow
ow	cow, now
ab	crab, dab
ib	crib, fib
ob	job, mob
ack	jack, snack
ike	like, bike

Match the letter

Topic
Any topic

Resources
- Match the letter templates on pages 173–175
- Thin card
- Scissors
- Laminator (optional)
- Felt-tipped pens
- Flip chart or easel or board

Learning objectives
- To match and identify letters
- To link sounds to letters, naming and sounding letters of the alphabet
- To hear and say initial and ending sounds in words

Preparation
- Photocopy the Match the letter templates (pages 173–175) on to thin card. Cut into cards. Laminate them if you wish.

What to do
- Write a letter on the flip chart or board. Ask the children what sound the letter makes.

Invite the children to take turns to find the matching letter from the 'alphabet bank' of letters on cards. If the children have an 'alphabet bank' set of letter cards each, ask them all to find the matching letter as quickly as they can.

Extensions/variations
- When the children know all their letter sounds, make capital letter cards and play the game with them.
- Look for letters that begin or end words that you are familiarizing the children with during other activities.

Misfit words

Learning objective
- To hear and say initial sounds, identifying similarities and differences within lists of words

What to do
- Explain to the children that you are going to give them groups of words; they must listen carefully and put up their hands to tell you which word in the group begins with a different sound from the others. Call out a series of words that begin with the same initial sound, including one word that begins with something different – for example: *bag*, *bed*, *ball*, *chair*, *banana*.

Extension/variation
- Ask the children to become leaders – they need to give at least three words beginning with the same sound and one with a different one. At first, they will probably always leave the misfit till the end. Try to encourage them to think about this before they decide on their words.

Topic
Any topic

Resources
- No special requirements

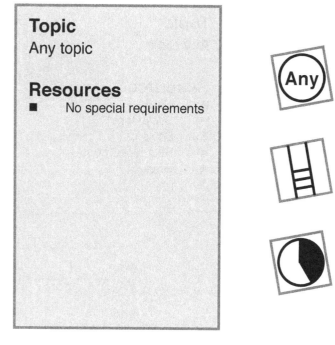

Pocket letters

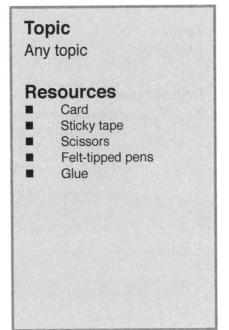

Topic
Any topic

Resources
- Card
- Sticky tape
- Scissors
- Felt-tipped pens
- Glue

Learning objective
● To link sounds to letters, naming and sounding letters of the alphabet

Preparation
● Make a display out of the card, giving it 26 pockets. Make these pockets look like little beds. Mark each bed with a letter of the alphabet (lower case). Make 26 small cards which will fit into the pockets; mark each one with a letter of the alphabet (lower case).

What to do
● Show the children the display. Talk about the alphabet and letter sounds, to familiarize them with this vocabulary. Remember not to add the 'uh' when you are making the sounds of letters.
● Show the children the cards. Suggest that they take turns to put a card to bed in its appropriate pocket.

● Hold up each card, ask the children what sound they think it says and choose a child to match it with its 'bed' and place it in the pocket.

Extensions/variations
● When the children are familiar with single letters, make 'beds' for double and cluster sounds, such as 'ch', 'br', 'st', 'str'.
● Develop this strategy by using whole words instead of letters, using children's name cards, or other key words that they are familiar with. These can be words from their favourite books or the names of things that have labels in your setting, or weather, or dinosaurs, or any other words you think the children will know.

I can ...

Learning objectives
● To hear, identify and say the initial words in sounds
● To link sounds to letters and to name and sound the letters of the alphabet
● To begin to understand the concept of alphabetical order

What to do
● This is a game that can be played over and over again. The children take turns, in order.
● Ask the first child to tell everyone something that she can do beginning with 'a' – for example, *act*. The next child thinks of something she can do beginning with 'b' – for example, *bite*. Keep going throughout the alphabet. You might have to leave some letters out if they prove too difficult (or make up some silly words!). If you have been through the alphabet once and have started again, you can't accept the same words.

Extensions/variations
● Change the theme so that, for example, instead of thinking of something they can *do*, the children think of something they can eat or drink, or something they can see.
● Sing the alphabet song.

Topic
Any topic

Resources
■ No special requirements

Silly sentences

Topic
Any topic

Resources
- Paper
- Felt-tipped pens

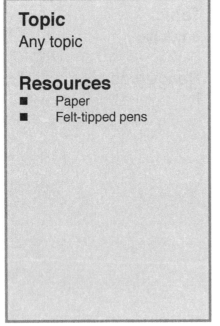

Learning objectives
- To hear and say initial sounds in words
- To link sounds to letters
- To develop an awareness of alliteration

Preparation
- Have the children sitting together, ready to concentrate.

What to do
- Tell the children the rhyme 'Peter Piper picked…' (see page 181).
- Ask them if they think you could all make up some silly sentences together. Invite them to choose a sound that they would like to have a go with to begin. Write the letter sound on one of the pieces of paper and show it to the children. Say the sound, and ask them to say it back to you. Make sure they do not add the 'uh' sound.

- Ask the children if they can think up a silly sentence. Give them a simple one to start with – for example, for the 's' sound, *Sam said sausages*, or *Sardines sing silly songs*, etc.
- Play this game in any odd minutes, ideally covering all the letter sounds over a period of time.

Extensions/variations
- Write out the silly sentences and ask the children to illustrate them for a display.
- Go on to double consonants and consonant clusters when you feel it will work. For example:
  - ◆ *Pretty princesses have no prickles.*
  - ◆ *Clever clocks clatter.*
  - ◆ *Straight streets stretch.*

© Irene Yates
www.brilliantpublications.co.uk

Echoes

Learning objectives
- To listen to and reproduce rhythmic sound patterns
- To recognize rhythm in spoken words and phrases

What to do
- Sit with the children and invite them to play a game. Clap a simple pattern and ask a child to clap it back to you. Repeat this for each child in turn. Invite them to take turns to clap a pattern of their own and to choose someone to clap it back to them, like an echo.

Extensions/variations
- Clap the rhythms of simple phrases – such as: 'How are you today?' and ask the children to try to guess what the phrases are.
- Clap the rhythms of other rhymes and songs that the children know.

Related activities
- Copy me (see page 49)
- Clapping the pattern (see page 28)

Topic
Any topic

Resources
- No special requirements

Naming names

Topic
Myself

Resources
■ Cards with the children's names on

Learning objective
● To recognize and read names

Preparation
● Make sure the children have had the chance to familiarize themselves with the name cards of everyone in the group.

What to do
● Tell the children that they are going to play a name game, called 'Naming names'. Take the children's name cards and spread them all out, in random directions, face up on a flat surface. Ask the children to take turns to find the card with their own name on it and pick it up. (It is interesting to see which children can still recognize their names even if the letters aren't the right way up, and which children can't see them if they appear to be upside down.)

● When all the cards are collected, take them back and mix them up. Put them out on the surface again. Give a child's name, and ask for someone else to find it. The child whose name it is can look but not touch or show where it is – until the other children have had a chance to recognize and take it.

Extensions/variations
● Play the same game with different words – eg, words the children are fairly familiar with from their books or DVDs or from environmental print.
● Use words familiar to the children, appropriate to other key areas, for example in maths you might use the names of specific shapes.

Related activity
● Know-a-name (see page 113)

Know-a-name

Learning objective
● To recognize and read names

Preparation
● Make sure all the children know each other's names. Make a name card for each child and adult in the group.
● Hold up one card at a time. Ask the children whose name it is. Hopefully, the child whose name it is will recognize it. If not, give clues, such as '… it begins with the sound of… .' When making the sounds, give a clear sound without an 'uh' ending – for instance say 'sssss' not 'suh'.
● Give each card to the appropriate child. Give them lots of opportunity to share their cards with each other, showing, talking, comparing and contrasting. For example, you can say things like, 'Whose name has got a 'h' sound in it?' etc.
● Collect the cards in for another time.

Extensions/variations
● Make sure that all the adults in the group have a name card as well, and share them with the children.
● Play a game that involves giving name cards to children and asking them to read the names and give them to the right people
● Encourage the children to write their own names and notice others' names on all of their pieces of work.

Related activity
● Naming names (see page 112).

Topic
Myself

Resources
■ Cards with the children's names written on
■ Felt-tipped pen

Chant a story

Topic
Any topic

Resources
- A collection of stories and books with which the children are familiar
- Large format ('big') books

Learning objectives
- To listen to and join in with stories and poems
- To recognize rhythm in spoken words
- To begin to read words and simple sentences

What to do
- Try to find big books with lots of recurring phrases and strong rhythms that the children enjoy. Read the same familiar stories over and over again. Encourage the children to chant along with you as you read, by pointing to different words and pictures. They will begin to associate some of the words with some of the pictures and they will begin to rote-read the passages with you. Eventually they will start to recognize some of the words and phrases and you will be able to remain silent whilst pointing to the words so that the children take over the reading.

Extension/variation
- Encourage the children to share the books in pairs and chant-read them together without any help from you.

Make a necklace

Learning objectives
- To read and understand short sentences
- To attempt to write words and short sentences to create simple instructions
- To develop hand/eye coordination
- To demonstrate good control in small movements and manipulation of materials

What to do
- Show the children how to make a necklace by threading breakfast cereal on to the wool or string. Tie the ends making sure that the necklaces will go over the children's heads.
- Tell the children that you would like to write some instructions for other children on how to make the necklaces.
- Ask the children to help you to compose a title for the instructions. The instructions need to be in two parts, *What you need* and *What you do.* Write down the first heading, reading the words back with the children. Take suggestions from them for the list and scribe them, reading the words back with the children. Write the second heading and repeat the process.
- Encourage children to add to the lists by writing the words and sentences that they choose, at their own level of writing ability, offering support when needed.

Extensions/variations
- Invite the children to explain to other children or adults how they made their necklaces.
- Ask the children to 'read' their instructions to other children or adults.
- Use this technique to support the children in writing instructions for other things, such as how to feed the guinea pig, etc.

Topic
Any topic

Resources
- Pieces of string or wool
- Breakfast cereal with holes in
- Flip chart
- Felt-tipped pen

Print walk

Topic
Gardening/environment

Resources
- Large sheet of paper on flip chart or easel
- Felt-tipped pens
- Clipboards, paper and pencils to make notes while out walking

 Ensure correct adult : child ratios.

Learning objective
- To show interest in and understanding of print in the environment

Preparation
- Have the children ready to go for a walk.

What to do
- Tell the children that you are going out for a walk and that it is a special kind of walk because you are going to look for all the things you can see that have words printed – in other words, *writing*.
- Encourage the children to look for road signs, road names, shop names, house names, notices in shop windows, advertisements, billboards, etc.
- Every time they see one, give them praise and help them to 'read' it, encouraging them to give you any of the sounds that they can see. Read the word/s then ask them to repeat them to you and read them again together.
- When you get back to your setting, talk about all the print that you saw, ask the children what they can remember and make a list of it for them on the flip chart, which you can then 'read' back together.

Extensions/variations
- Make a set of road signs, road names and shop names and build up a small locality for role-play activities.
- Look for specific street print – for instance, if you are doing a project on 'water', look for a 'Swimming Pool' sign or a 'No swimming in the lake' sign, etc.

Links to home
- Ask for parent helpers to go on the walk.

Shopping trip

Reading

Learning objectives
- To know that print carries meaning
- To read a range of familiar and common words independently

Preparation
- Find two of each item of grocery, eg cereal packets, toothpaste packets, tissue boxes, milk powder cans, etc. Cut the label from one packet and put the other packet in the large box or set them up in your shopping area. Glue the cut out labels to pieces of card to make them more sturdy.

What to do
- Give each child a shopping bag. Share out the labels between them. Tell the children that the labels which they have are their own shopping list. What you want them to do is go to the shop, or box, and find the items which they have labels for.
- When they bring back their shopping in the bags, ask them to sort out each packet and match it to its label. Encourage the children to read the labels on the packets, using the pictures as clues.

Extension/variation
- Play a shopping game with all the children. Have them sitting in a circle and the packets on display somewhere in the room. Hold out the labels, upside down so that the children don't know which is which. Invite each child in turn to take a label, then look around the room to find the right packet and bring it back to the circle. Reward the children with praise, stickers or whatever you prefer for matching and reading the packets correctly.

Topic
Food and shopping

Resources
- Grocery packets
- Scissors
- Card
- Glue
- Shopping bags
- Large box

Re-tell a story

Topic
Any topic

Resources
- A3 sheets of coloured paper
- Lots of A6 paper (A4 cut into quarters)
- Felt-tipped pens
- Crayons
- Glue
- Hole punch
- Ring clips or treasury tags

Learning objectives
- To be aware of the way stories are structured
- To describe story settings, events and principal characters and draw pictures to represent them
- To attempt to write words, captions and simple sentences to communicate meaning
- To use talk to organize, sequence and clarify ideas and events, and to develop a storyline connecting them

Preparation
- Choose a story the children know and love.

What to do
- Talk about the chosen story. Encourage the children to remember all the main events and put them into the right order. Suggest that together you make a book, telling the story.
- Give each child a piece of A6 paper and invite her to draw a picture illustrating what she chooses as the first event.
- Select some of the pictures to stick to the first right-hand page. Ask the children to help you decide on text for the left-hand page. Keep it very simple, one or two sentences

only, and write it in large text, saying the words as you write.
- Model where you start and the direction you write in. Explain the full stop(s) at the end(s) of the sentence(s).
- Repeat these steps until you get to the end of the story. Ensure that you choose a selection of each child's pictures and include them on enough different pages, so that everyone's work is represented fairly.
- When the pages are finished, number them with the children's help. Decide on a title and authorship for the cover page.
- Check that the events and words are in the right order, punch holes down the left-hand side and secure the pages with ring clips or treasury tags. (You can use string or wool but it will not be quite so strong. Make sure that you tie two separate pieces of string, loosely enough, through the top and bottom holes, if you would like the pages to lie flat.)

Extensions/variations
- Read the book with individuals, pairs or small groups.
- Make the book available for the children to share when they wish.
- Make a book yourself of a story the children love, and introduce it to them.

Links to home
- Encourage the children to take the book home to share with their parents.

Book words

Learning objective
● To use vocabulary and forms of speech increasingly influenced by experience of books

Preparation
● Discuss with the children the idea of making a book. Decide together on a suitable subject for the book, such as 'Our walk to the shops.

What to do
● Ask the children to tell you the various things that a book needs. You are aiming for them to use words such as:
  ◆ Cover
  ◆ Title
  ◆ Author
  ◆ Illustrator
  ◆ Pages
  ◆ Back
  ◆ Front
  ◆ Words
  ◆ Letters
  ◆ Pictures
  ◆ Numbers (on pages).
● Decide how many pages your book will have. Add a front cover and a back cover. Secure the covers and pages.
● Invite each group to make some pictures and some words for two pages. Use book vocabulary all the time and encourage children to become familiar with it and use it confidently.
● When all the pages are finished, gather the groups together to decide on a title and how you will show who the authors and illustrators were. Model writing the names.

Topic
Any topic

Resources
■ Lots of books
■ A4 paper and card
■ Ring clips
■ Hole punch
■ Pens
■ Pencils

● Number the pages.
● Read the book with the children, asking questions that will elicit book vocabulary.

Extension/variation
● When reading books with the children, use the vocabulary confidently and naturally, showing the children that you expect them to use the words in future discussions.

Related activity
● Book know-how (see page 96)

Feel free book

Topic
Any topic

Resources
- Paper
- Pens
- Crayons
- Pencils
- Scissors
- Coloured paper
- Sticky tape
- Hole punch
- String
- Staples
- Glue
- Arts and craft items and recycled pieces such as card, fabrics, foam, cellophane, tissue paper, buttons, beads, sequins, ribbons, stickers, etc

Learning objectives
- To understand and use the vocabulary and structure of books
- To create pictures and words and link them together to tell a story or provide information
- To handle and manipulate materials and tools effectively
- To safely use and explore techniques and express ideas and thoughts imaginatively

Preparation
- Have a 'making books' table laid out with all of the book-making materials, supplies, equipment and resources. It will help if the children have made books with you before.

What to do
- Suggest to the children that they each make a book. Their book can be any kind of book they like, and they can make it about anything they want to make it about. Don't set any guidelines, let them treat the activity freely – as a kind of problem-solving exercise.
- As the children set about making their books, discuss the implications:
  - What do you want your book to look like?
  - How do you want to fix it together?
  - What do you want your book to be about?
  - Will it have pictures?
  - Will it have words?
  - Will you have to stick things in? What will you stick in?
  - Where will the pictures be?
  - Where will the words be?
  - Do you want to put numbers on the pages?
  - What will go on the cover?
- Encourage the children to work as independently and creatively as possible while drawing and writing, and encourage discussion and conversation throughout the activity. Remember to observe, wait and listen to give them the optimum opportunity for describing the task as they perform it.
- When all the books are finished, invite the children to read and share them with each other. Offer lots of praise and encouragement.

Extensions/variations
- Make a display of all the books.
- Encourage individual children to share their books with other children and with other adults.

Links to home
- Encourage parents to make books with the children at home.

© Irene Yates
www.brilliantpublications.co.uk

Print a book

Learning objectives
- To listen to and join in with stories
- To begin to recognize letters and words and read simple sentences
- To know that information can be retrieved from books and from computers
- To recognize that technology is used in places such as homes, schools and nurseries

What to do
- First, create a story with the children. Make it simple, and include some of the concepts that the children are learning, such as colours, days of the week, numbers, etc. For example:

  On Monday we do painting.
  On Tuesday we go for a walk.
  On Wednesday we play in the sand.
  On Thursday we make biscuits.
  On Friday we read some stories.
  On Saturday we stay in bed.
  On Sunday we get ready for
  *   tomorrow...*

- Use one page for each sentence. Choose a large font so that the children identify any letters they may be able to recognize.
- Type out a title page for the story, showing the children's names as authors.
- Print the story and secure the pages together. Invite the children to illustrate the text by drawing pictures on separate pieces of paper, cutting them out and sticking them onto the book pages, beside the words.

Extensions/variations
- Make several different books with several groups of children, including various concepts they are learning.
- Keep the books together in a display so that the children can share them with each other.

Links to home
- Encourage the children to take the books home to share with their families.

Topic
Any topic

Resources
- Computer
- Word-processing program
- Graphics program
- Printer
- Paper

Send an e-mail

Topic
Any topic

Resources
- Computer
- Internet link
- e-mail address(es) of people prepared to correspond with children by e-mail

Hello Sarah, what are you doing today?

Learning objectives
- To read and understand simple sentences
- To demonstrate understanding when talking with others about what has been read
- To write short sentences in meaningful contexts
- To understand how and why people send and receive messages by email

Preparation
- Make sure you have introduced the children to the computer (see page 22).

What to do
- When the children have written letters to each other and to other people, introduce them to the idea of sending an e-mail. Explain that an e-mail is very much like a letter; it is a message you send to somebody else but instead of putting it into an envelope and posting it in the post box for the post delivery person to deliver, you send it yourself, via a mail server, from one computer to another.
- Decide on the person who is to receive the e-mail. Set the e-mail up yourself, explaining

what you are doing. Make sure you are using a large-sized font so that the children can 'read' it. Discuss what your message should be. Let the children have a turn in keying in some of the message with your help. When you have read the message back together and the children are satisfied, let one of them click on 'send'.
- With the children, check that the recipient received the e-mail and await a reply.

Extension/variation
- Make sending and receiving e-mails a regular activity. You could join forces with another group to do this.

Links to home
- Find out if there are any parents willing to swap e-mails with the group occasionally.

© Irene Yates
www.brilliantpublications.co.uk

Writing

- The earliest stages of writing development are known as 'emergent writing'. Children may begin to make 'scribble writing' and to allocate messages to their scribbles because they understand that written symbols give messages and that writing and drawing are two different things. They may sometimes make letters that can be deciphered and they may also begin to write or copy their own names.

- Children move on to 'experimental writing', which looks more like real writing but still doesn't make any sense. They now understand that speech can be written down and that the message will stay the same once it is written in symbols. They also begin to see that, in English, the symbols are read from left to right and down the page. They experiment with writing real letters and words and can usually read their own messages. Eventually, it may be possible for adults to work out what some of the words are.

- While children are developing their emergent writing skills, adults can support them by providing opportunities for copying and tracing or by modelling the writing process when scribing messages for them. It is important to ask children what they would like to write and then to show them how to write it and help them to read it back. Describing how to write letters (eg, down, up, round and into the middle, etc), and asking questions about the words and sounds being used (eg, Which sound does it begin with? How do we write that?), demonstrate for children the different thought processes involved in writing.

- After the emergent writing stage, children continue to develop their skills, beginning to understand the way letters need to be formed and that spelling is important. They then move on to using punctuation and planning their writing. Making marks during the Foundation Stage enables children to practise their writing skills, while positive feedback and encouragement from adults motivates them to want to become proficient writers.

- Making books with children gives them a reason to want to write and to read what they have written. They will develop their literacy skills through much practice and through proudly sharing their own books with others.

● Children can record important events and experiences in their own books, extending both their literacy and their communication skills by selecting materials, planning and deciding upon pictures and words and then enjoying their books together. The role of the adults is to ensure that a variety of papers and tools for writing and drawing are always available for independent work and also to offer pictures to cut out, opportunities to take photographs and continuous support and encouragement.

Do these words rhyme?

Learning objectives
- To identify both rhyming and non-rhyming words
- To segment sounds and blends within simple words and create rhyming strings of real and imaginary words

Preparation
- Prepare in advance some lists of words that rhyme. To each list of rhyming words, add one word that doesn't rhyme (see examples in the box).
- Children should be sitting quietly and ready to listen.

What to do
- Say the words clearly and slowly to the children and ask them to identify the word which doesn't fit the rhyming pattern.
- Make sure you don't always give the rhyming and non-rhyming words in the same order. Also, stick to short, one-syllable words, but vary the way you make them 'not rhyme'. For instance, you may have the same middle vowel, but a different sound ending, or you may have a completely different vowel sound and the same ending.
- Support children as they write their own lists of rhyming words and find out which ones can be found just by changing the initial letter and which ones are spelt differently.

Extension/variation
- Give the children the set of rhyming words and ask for volunteers to give you words that don't rhyme. Ask the children if they can find rhyming words for the new 'non-rhyming' words.

Related activities
- Silly words (see page 105)
- Rhyming names (see page 31)

Topic
Any topic

Resources
- Prepared list of rhyming words

Lists you could use (the non-rhyming words are underlined):

cat, hat, <u>dot</u>, mat

by, fly, tie, <u>tin</u>

toe, no, <u>note</u>, row

sea, <u>ship</u>, flea, tree

day, play, <u>why</u>, say

hair, bear, pear, <u>pin</u>

door, four, more, <u>rain</u>

boy, toy, <u>girl</u>, joy

slow, grow, toe, <u>tooth</u>

blue, threw, shoe, <u>ball</u>

track, back, <u>front</u>, Jack

lob, sob, <u>dish</u>, rob

Make a sound book

Topic
Any topic

Resources
- A3 paper or card
- Old catalogues/ magazines
- Glue
- Scissors
- Felt-tipped pens
- Ring clips
- Hole punch

Learning objectives
- To link sounds to letters, naming and sounding letters of the alphabet
- To hear and say the initial sounds in words
- To write recognizable letters, forming them correctly

Preparation
- Make this book after you have done some work on 'beginning' sounds.

What to do
- Suggest to the children that they make a book of things beginning with the same sound. Discuss which sound they would like to work on and come to an agreement.
- Look for things in the catalogues/magazines which begin with the chosen sound. Cut out and stick a few items to each page. As the children are working on the task, keep reinforcing the sound and its shape.
- Help the children to finger-trace the letter in the air.

- On the cover, write the title: *Our book of 's' things* (or whichever sound they are doing), and an authorship.
- Number the pages with the children, reminding them that you do not have a number on the cover or inside cover and that page 1 is the first right-hand page.
- Punch holes and secure.
- Read the book with the children, naming and talking about the things on their pages.

Extension/variation
- Work on many different single letters over a period of time, both consonants and vowels. Eventually, move on with more able children to work on double consonants (such as 'll') and clusters (such as 'str', cl).

I-spy alphabet book

Learning objectives
- To link sounds to letters, naming and sounding the letters of the alphabet
- To understand how to form letters correctly
- To hear and say initial sounds in words
- To absorb and remember alphabetical order

Preparation
- Make sure that the children are familiar with and able to play the game 'I-Spy'.
- On 26 sheets, write the words, *I spy with my little eye, something beginning with…*

What to do
- You will need the 26 pages and a page for the front cover of the book, though you might choose to do, say, three or four letters only in each session.
- On each page, with the children, read the words 'I spy…' and go through the alphabet (use a visual aid if you have one on display). Say the words together, then you write the letter. If you have introduced capitals, say the name and the sound, and write both. As you are writing, ask the children to trace the letters in the air, and ask them where you will start the letter.
- Take suggestions from the children for things they might be able to see beginning with the relevant letter in:
  - the rooms of the setting
  - their home
  - the park
  - the shops
  and write them on the appropriate page.
- At the end of the session, talk again about the letters you have covered and remind the children of the things they identified.

Extensions/variations
- Ask the children to draw or cut out pictures to stick into the alphabet book.
- Reinforce memory and understanding of alphabetical order by reading through the pages of the book in order.

Topic
Gardening and environment

Resources
- Sugar paper
- Ring clips or treasury tags
- Paper to draw on
- Scissors
- Glue
- Felt-tip pens

I spy with my little eye, something beginning with…
d

Scribble scribble

Topic
Any topic

Resources
- Large pieces of paper
- Big writing tools like fat crayons and fat felt-tipped pens that do not need a lot of pressure in order to make marks
- Chubby pencils
- Rubber pencil grips for the children that need them

Learning objectives
- To give meaning to marks made while scribbling, drawing and writing
- To develop hand/eye coordination
- To develop fine motor control
- To handle equipment and tools effectively, including pencils for writing

Preparation
- Have all the materials ready, with the paper on a flat or slanted surface. Sometimes it helps children if the paper is at an angle so that they do not have to use too much pressure with the tools.
- Help the children to hold the writing tools correctly.
- Accept right- or left-handed use of tools.

What to do
- Encourage the children to experiment with random and uncontrolled scribbling, making indiscriminate marks on the surface of the paper. Encourage movements in all directions – up/down, down/up, right/left, left/right, diagonally – whatever the child feels happy to do. Use the vocabulary of different directions so that the children absorb the language.
- Give plenty of time for them to explore.
- Ask: 'Is it a picture? What is it of? Is it writing? What does it say?' Listen attentively for each child's comments on their own work.
- Show the children how you write their names (pointing out letters and sounds where appropriate) and the date on their 'writing'.

Extensions/variations
- Start a collection of dated 'writing' for each child and add to it every two weeks or so. This will enable you to keep a Record of Achievement and to follow the child's progress.
- Suggest topics to the children that fit in with other areas that you are exploring. For example, if you have been looking at mini-beasts you could say, 'Why don't you write about the snails we saw?'

Controlled scribble

Learning objectives
- To give meaning to marks while drawing scribbling and writing
- To use anti-clockwise movement and retrace vertical lines
- To develop hand/eye coordination
- To develop fine motor control
- To handle tools effectively and use a pencil to form recognizable letters

Preparation
- Have the writing tools all ready, with the paper on a flat or slanted surface.

What to do
- Observe how the children move from uncontrolled scribbling to more controlled efforts.
- Encourage left to right movements.
- Encourage circle shapes, straight lines and squiggly lines.
- Use the language of writing symbols and shapes, such as 'round', 'upwards', 'downwards', 'straight', 'squiggly', 'dot', 'top', 'bottom', etc.
- Ask: 'What are you going to draw/write? Where will you start? Which way will your pen/crayon go?'
- Give the children plenty of time to explore what they can do.
- When the children have finished, discuss their writing/drawing with them. Let them see you writing on their product, 'This is (name)'s picture of...' or '(name)'s story says...'. Read your words back to them, pointing to them as you read.

Extensions/variations
- Add to the collection of each child's pieces.
- Link to other areas by suggesting content that ties in with topics you are exploring currently with the children.

Topic
Any topic

Resources
- Large pieces of paper
- Large writing tools: felt-tipped pens, crayons, paintbrushes, etc

Special writing

Topic
Any topic

Resources
- Large sheet of paper
- Coloured felt-tipped pens
- Small piece of card
- Black felt-tipped pens

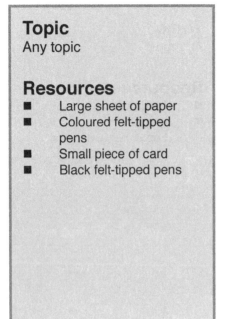

Learning objective
- To practise mark making and writing skills at all individual levels

Preparation
- Put the sheet of paper on a writing surface, with lots of coloured felt tipped pens.

What to do
- Tell the children that you would like them to make a big writing display to put on the wall for the parents to see. They may say that they 'cannot write' but emphasize that you want them to do their own special kind of writing and that they may write or make marks in any way that they wish to.
- Invite the children to choose their own colours and the writing that they would like to do, and to work independently. The writing may turn out to be squiggles or letters or scribbles, but it will all be acceptable for the display.

- Write a caption on the card, showing the names of the children and reporting that they 'did all of this writing'. Display it in a prominent place. Look at it with the rest of the children and read the caption to them.

Extensions/variations
- Give the children opportunities to experiment with writing in outside situations – either on paper and card or on paving slabs and other surfaces, so that they understand that print can happen in all places, not just inside on a table or desk!
- When you have studied a specific topic, ask children to write 'about it' in the same way; change your caption to read 'x and x did all this writing about … (whatever the topic is)'.

© Irene Yates
www.brilliantpublications.co.uk

Over-copying

Learning objectives

- To write labels, captions and simple sentences
- To read and understand words and simple sentences
- To develop skills in over-copying, or tracing over, writing
- To use a pencil and hold it effectively to form recognizable letters, most of which are correctly formed

Preparation

- Talk about something that the children have been doing, or something that has been happening in the group, or a story that you have shared with them, so that the children have an idea of something that they could compose a 'story' about.

What to do

- Recap the event with the children and ask them to each think about how they could illustrate it. Give the children paper and time to create their own pictures. Ask them to think about the text that might go with their pictures. Help each child to put her ideas into one or more sentences.
- Work with each child individually. Scribe, in light pencil and big letters, the sentence(s) or caption(s) that she has composed, demonstrating how to form the letters and where to leave spaces. Show where to start each letter and which directions to move the pencil in and read the words aloud. The children should know exactly what they are over-copying and be able to attempt to read the text back for themselves.
- Give each child time to over-copy, or trace, their composed text, and help them to read it back again, then have a sharing time when each child shares their story with the rest of the small group.

Extensions/variations

- Instead of doing 'light' pencil work, write a dotted version for the children to go over. Alternatively use a highlighter pen.

Topic
Any topic

Resources
- Paper
- Pencils
- Felt-tipped pens
- Highlighter pens

- Write out the children's favourite nursery rhymes for them to trace and illustrate. They can take them home, make a display of them, or turn them into a nursery rhyme book.

Copy-writing

Topic
Any topic

Resources
- Paper
- Writing implements

Learning objective
- To copy words in order, to learn to write names, labels, captions and sentences

Preparation
- Set up activities that will give the children opportunities for writing, for example playing post offices, schools, etc.

What to do
- Sit with the child, discussing what needs to be written, which may be a sentence, a caption, or a list. Make it relevant to the activity the child is taking part in.
- Draw a line across the sheet of paper. Ask the child to dictate to you what she wants to write. Write the child's message carefully and slowly across the top half of the paper, making sure you leave noticeable gaps between words. Leave space for copying below; the child needs to be able to copy each letter/word underneath. If you write more than one line, make sure there is space to copy the first line before you start the next line. Read the message back with the child, pointing to the words as you go along.

- Show the child where to copy, and let her write independently. Try not to intervene as it is important at this stage that she carries out the task with confidence and feels that she is able to do it. However, take note of how she is forming the different letters and, if any of the movements are wrong, find opportunities during other times and activities to model correct letter formations, to avoid bad habits being formed and letters becoming less recognizable.
- Read the child's message back with her.

Extensions/variations
- Use the copying technique for short messages. Don't expect the child to try to copy long pieces of text.
- Use the copying technique for children to learn to write their own names.
- When they have developed good copying skills, offer longer texts of two or three sentences.

Marks for meaning

Learning objectives
- To give meaning to marks for the purpose of labelling equipment
- To hear and say initial sounds, segment sounds and blend them together and know which letters represent some of them, in order to write words and simple sentences
- To read, understand and use the written labels when taking tools and equipment or putting things away

Preparation
- Mix up some of the equipment, so that it needs to be sorted into its appropriate sets.

What to do
- Ask the children to help you sort out the tools or equipment. Ask them how you and they could be sure that when anyone uses them they would all go into the right place. Guide them towards the suggestion that if boxes, drawers, etc were labelled then everyone would know where everything should go.
- Suggest that you write new labels together for the sets you have made.
- Ask the children to suggest what the labels should say. Rather than just 'pencils' (for example), encourage them to think of a sentence such as 'Put the pencils in here.'
- Write each label carefully, with the children observing. Ask children to show you how to form the letters that they know, by writing them with their fingers in the air (see Sky-writing, page 136). Encourage children to write their own labels, either independently or with support, spelling the words correctly by copying them or checking the letters with an adult.
- At the end of the session, read back all the labels, carefully, with the children.

Extensions/variations
- Write one-word labels, eg 'pencils', 'crayons', 'balls', etc. Encourage children to match the items with the words on the labels.

Topic
Any topic

Resources
- Toy and tool boxes, shelves, drawers, etc where you store the equipment used with the group
- Card
- Writing implements

- Encourage the children to 'read' the labels when putting things away. They will probably recognize the right container from other cues, but reinforcing the written words each time helps to reinforce phonic knowledge and reading and writing skills.

Modelling writing

Topic
Any topic

Resources
- Paper
- Writing implements

- ◆ that there are gaps between words
- ◆ that the words say the same thing no matter how many times we read them.
- If you 'model' the writing as you are doing it, the children pick up these concepts without even knowing it.
- For example, if you were writing a child's name, you would say, 'What sound does it begin with? Where shall we start? Which way shall we go? How do we do this letter? We do a line down, a line across for the T. What's the next sound? It's an "o". We start here and go backwards and round. What's the last sound? It's a "mmm"' (try not to say 'muh'.), *'To do a "m" we start here, go down, go up and over, down again, up and over and down.'*
- It isn't necessary to model every single piece of writing, but lots of consistent modelling allows children to absorb the basic concepts and gives them the confidence to attempt to write for themselves.

Learning objective
- To understand how to write and the reasons for and uses of writing

Preparation
- Set up activities that give you the opportunity to model, or demonstrate, writing, such as making books, writing stories, writing lists, writing notes, etc.

What to do
- Important points for writing for children to learn at this stage are:
  - ◆ that, in English, we write in a left to right direction
  - ◆ that sounds and shapes (letters) are connected
  - ◆ that we always write the shapes (letters) in the same way

Extension/variation
- Use modelling to write group pieces, and always ask the children to read the writing back to you when you have composed a piece together.

Multicultural link
- Some languages are not written from left to right (eg, Arabic, Hebrew, Chinese). Collect examples of different alphabets and pieces of writing in languages that are read in other directions. If you have families who read and write in these languages at home, encourage parents to come into the setting to demonstrate for the children, to provide examples of writing or to lend books, magazines or newspapers.

Sand-writing

Learning objectives
- To learn and practise correct letter formation
- To link sounds to letters
- To demonstrate good control of fine movements and begin to form recognizable letters

What to do
- Show the children how they might draw pictures or write letters in the sand with a finger. Encourage them to experiment with writing different letter sounds that they know. Model for them how to form the letters with a finger in the air first so that they are sure where the letters start and end.

- Invite them to explore the differences between writing in the wet sand and in the dry sand. Ask them questions such as: 'What happens to the sand? How different does it feel to your finger? Do the letters stay the same? Could we write our names in the sand? Would we be able to write a whole message in the sand? Would it be the same as writing a message on paper? Why? What would happen to it?'

- Help them to write their own names and their friends' names so that they are learning and practising a wide range of different letters.

Extension/variation
- Experiment with making letters in different ways. Help the children to shape letters out of dough or Plasticine, or draw them onto coloured paper and cut them out.

Topic
Any topic

Resources
- Wet and/or dry sand trays
- Dough or Plasticine
- Coloured paper
- Scissors
- Pencils

Sky-writing

Topic
Any topic

Resources
- No special requirements

Learning objectives
- To practise letter shapes
- To use some clearly identifiable letters, formed in the correct way
- To demonstrate good control and coordination in large and small movements

Preparation
- Introduce this activity at any time once the children have begun to build up their knowledge of letter shapes.

What to do
- Have the children sitting or standing in a group with you standing in front of them. Tell them you are going to show them how to do *sky-writing*, which is writing letters in the air with a finger.
- Choose a child's name to write in the air.
- You need to stand with your back to the children so that you are all facing the same way. Ask the children what sound the child's name begins with. Write it in the air, describing it as you go, for example, 'Shazia's name begins with S, the sound "s". We start at the top, go backwards and round, then forwards and round and backwards again.'
- Repeat the first letter, then go on to the next one, and so on.

Extensions/variations
- When the children are used to making letters, ask them to make them as big as they can, using their whole arm and shoulder instead of just one finger.
- Then ask the children to make the letters as tiny as they can, as though on their thumbnail. All the time, verbalize the correct way to form the letter shape.
- Encourage the children to say the direction words to themselves quietly when they are using writing tools on paper.

Related activity
- Write it right! (see page 139)

Chalk-a-line

Learning objectives

- To give meaning to marks while drawing and writing
- To handle and manipulate tools effectively, to write and draw
- To develop control and coordination in large and small movements
- To recognize some numerals
- To realize that steps and jumps can be counted and to develop counting skills through playing a game

Preparation

- Make sure the children know which area they are allowed to use the chalk in.

What to do

- Show the children how to draw shapes, lines and dots with the chalk. Just give them the opportunity to have fun drawing shapes or squiggly lines, walking along them, running from one dot or mark to another, and creating new images.
- The idea is to encourage them to enjoy making their own marks, and to develop a good flow, as well as freedom of expression.
- Use the spray bottle and cloth to clean up after you.

Extensions/variations

- As hand/eye coordination develops, suggest shapes for the children to draw and walk round, on or along.
- Draw a hopscotch area with numbers and show the children how to play.

Topic

Any topic

Resources

- Large floor or outside paved area
- Chalk
- Cloth and spray bottle of water for cleaning up

Matching shapes

Topic
Shapes

Resources
- Coloured card
- Scissors

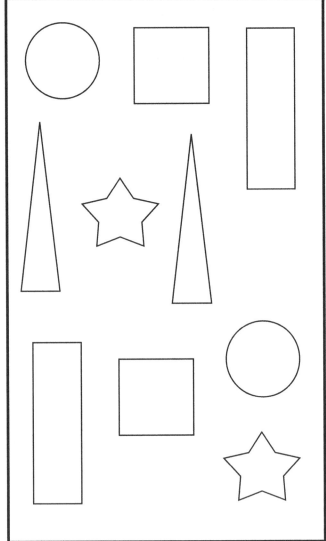

Learning objectives
- To distinguish between different marks and symbols and ascribe meaning to them
- To extend vocabulary by grouping and naming and by exploring the sounds of new words
- To use everyday language to talk about shape, size and colour and to compare objects and quantities

Preparation
- This activity will encourage the children to notice how all the shapes in a set are actually different from each other, which will lead them to observe how letters and words differ from one another.
- Cut out shapes, such as squares, rectangles, circles, stars and triangles in various sizes and colours.

What to do
- Mix up all the shapes. Ask the children to sort the pieces of card into sets according to shape only. Encourage the children to

discuss the idea of 'same' and 'different'. Talk about the colours and sizes and ask the children to describe to you what is different about the shapes.

Extension/variation
- Encourage the children to invent games with the shapes, so that they might have all the triangles together but laid out in size order, biggest first or smallest first – or lay them in sets of colours.

Communication and Language with Literacy

Write it right!

Learning objectives
● To learn and practise the writing of clearly identifiable letters
● To form letters correctly, in order to write neatly and in preparation for joined up handwriting later
● To handle equipment and tools effectively, including pencils for writing

Preparation
● Draw sets of three lines on paper. Two lines should be approximately 20mm apart and the third should be 7mm above the top line.
● Practise writing the letters yourself so that you know the exact movements. Use the template on page 176.

What to do
● It is important that the children learn the correct formation of the letters from the beginning. Once they have learned to form them incorrectly, by starting in the wrong place or moving the pencil in the wrong direction, it will be almost impossible for them to change their habits and re-learn the letters.
● They need to be taught that each whole letter is written in one go. The only letters for which they should take the pencil from the page before completing them are the k, the x, to dot the i and j and to cross the t and f.
● Make up little mantras to say with them as they are forming the letters. For example, for a, you might say, 'Start over here, backwards and round, down, round at the bottom, up, up, up (don't take your pencil off) and down again, add a little tail.' This will really help them to get fixed in their head how each letter should be formed.

Topic
Any topic

Resources
■ Paper
■ Thick pencils
■ Pencil grips
■ Rule
■ Forming letters template (see pages 176)

● Don't tackle too many letters at once. Start with the letters of their names and only add more letters as you see how they are progressing.

Extensions/variations
● Add capital letters only when the children need them, for example for their initials.
● More able children will be interested in the alphabet and its order, but others will not yet be ready to understand and should not be introduced to it too early.

Links to home
● If you can make an opportunity to show parents how letters should be formed, you will be giving the children lots of additional help. Perhaps you could run a 'Writing half-hour' to show them how important this is.

This is me

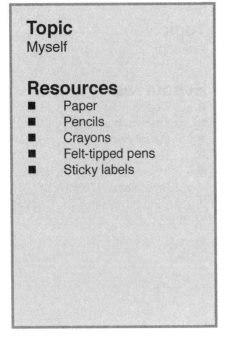

Topic
Myself

Resources
- Paper
- Pencils
- Crayons
- Felt-tipped pens
- Sticky labels

Learning objectives
- To use clearly identifiable letters to communicate meaning, representing sounds correctly and in sequence
- To learn and remember how to write own name
- To know which letters represent some sounds
- To use a pencil and hold it effectively to form recognizable letters, most of which are correctly formed

Preparation
- Have the paper and writing tools ready for the children to work with. At the top of each child's sheet, write 'This is me.' At the bottom of the sheet, write 'My name is' and a line for the child to write their name on.

What to do
- Explain to the children what the words at the top and bottom of the page say. Give them each a sticky label and tell them that this is for them to write their name on; when they are satisfied with their writing then they can stick the label in the appropriate space.
- Ask the children to draw a picture of themselves on the paper and colour it in. Go round the group, helping each child to write her name. Involve the children sitting close to her, by asking 'What sound does Emma's name begin with? Does anyone know how to write the letter? Where shall we start it?', etc.
- Make sure that the children are holding their pencils correctly; try to provide chubby pencils, triangular pencils or rubber pencil holders for any child who has problems with this. Decide which kind of writing would be best for each child – over-copying, copying, or verbal support.
- Encourage the children to learn the shapes of the letters of their name, as well as the sounds. Encourage them to compare their names and discover which letters are the same and which are different.
- Make a display of the self-portraits.

Extensions/variations
- Ask the children to draw and colour pictures for their parents and help them to write their own name on their work.
- Always ask children to write their names on pieces of artwork that they do in any area, until they begin to do so automatically.
- Help the children to develop the pincer movement they need to hold a pencil correct, by offering activities such as threading, sewing and cooking, or craft and play activities using lentils, sequins and other tiny pieces to manipulate.

Signing in

Learning objective
● To practise writing own name independently, or making marks to represent own name, to individual level of ability reached

Preparation
● Draw shapes on the sheet of card which are big enough for each child to write their name in.

What to do
● Tell the children that you sometimes do not know who's arrived and who hasn't because you are busy saying hello to other people or doing something else, but it would be very handy if the children could 'sign in' when they arrive at the group.
● Show them where you are going to put the card – it needs to be on a flat or slanted surface but not a wall. Discuss with them the possibility of the pen going missing and show them how you are going to tie it to the string and sticky-tape the string to the card, to keep the pen in one place.
● Invite the children to practise writing their name in a space – if they cannot do their name encourage them to make a mark that represents their name.
● It will only take a few minutes to make a new piece of card for each day. Draw different shapes to contain the names – clouds, circles, triangles, sheep, cats, etc, and when the children go home ask them if they can guess what the shapes might be for the next day.

Topic
Any topic

Resources
■ Large sheet of card
■ Black felt-tipped pen
■ String
■ Sticky tape

Extension/variation
● Have a card with each child's name written on it, and a box. Instead of writing their names, the children find their own name and place it in the box.

Related activity
● This is me (see page 140)

Writing notes

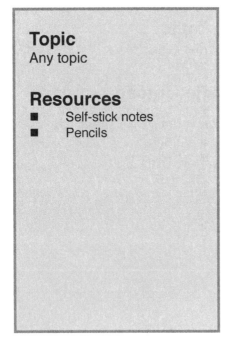

Topic
Any topic

Resources
- Self-stick notes
- Pencils

Learning objectives
- To attempt writing for different purposes – using different forms
- To be confident to try new activities and to say when needing or not needing help

Preparation
- Make some notes of your own on self-stick notes. It's useful to use self-stick notes when you are talking to or observing the children and you want to remind yourself of something you need to record later, instead of breaking off to do it immediately. Make notes on the self-stick notes, stick them in a space (wall or window) and collect them up at the end of the day. If the children see you doing this often they will become aware of the usefulness of notes.

What to do
- Explain to the children why you make your notes, so that you won't forget something important. Discuss how writing notes is not the same as writing stories, even though it is still writing and ask children if they can explain why. Tell the children that you are going to give them all some self-stick notes so that, during the session, they can make their own notes to remind them of things they want to tell you. Show them where to stick their notes. Write each child's name on the corner so that you know which belongs to whom. Give the children freedom to make the notes when they wish.
- At the end of the session, gather the notes and the children together. Invite one or two children to collect all the notes and hand them out to the appropriate children, asking for help to read the names when they need to.
- Invite each child to 'read' their notes to the group. Discuss the usefulness of the activity with them.

Extensions/variations
- Instead of leaving the children to 'write' their own notes, help them to write in whichever way is appropriate for their stage of development, ie scribbling, tracing, copying, etc.
- Help them to read the notes back.
- Use concepts from other areas as the focus points of specific notes. For example, say, 'Liam, could you write a note to remind us to check whether leaves turn gold in the autumn, please?'

Watch out!

Learning objective
● To write labels and captions and begin to form simple sentences

What to do
● When you are talking to the whole group, tell them that you are thinking about ideas for putting signs around your setting. For example, you may need a sign that says, 'Only two children in the water, please.' Ask the children to look around, while they are playing indoors and outside, to see if there is anywhere that needs a sign of any kind.
● Leave the card and the pen in a place that's accessible for the children and encourage them to have a go at making a sign when they find somewhere that needs one. When they have made a sign, they should read it to you.
● Encourage imaginative thinking and help the children to display their signs in appropriate places.

Extensions/variations
● Encourage the children to construct messages that are important to them – *'Don't scare the birds away, Don't climb the tree, No fighting for bikes'*, and so on.
● Help the children to formulate a range of rules for keeping safe and happy.

Related activity
● Marks for meaning (see page 133)

Topic
Any topic

Resources
■ Card
■ Felt-tipped pen

Colour words

Topic
Colours

Resources
- Sugar paper (different colours)
- Hole punch
- Ring clips
- White A4 paper
- Coloured felt-tipped pens
- Glue-stick
- Flip chart or white board

Learning objectives
- To hear and say initial sounds in words
- To write simple words and sentences

Preparation
- Use coloured sheets of sugar paper to make a book. Put the sheets together, punch two holes down one side and secure with ring clips. Write the title 'Our Colour Book' in assorted colours on white paper and stick it to the front cover.
- Gather the children together, to sit in a group to listen and join in.

What to do
- Discuss the colours of the pages.
- Ask the children to tell you the sound each colour begins with. Finger-trace the letters of the sounds in the air.
- Write the letters and then the words on a flip chart or white board.

- Give each child a sheet of white paper. Ask them to select a colour. Help them to trace, copy or write the sound their colour begins with on their paper, then go on to write the whole word. They could then draw a bubble around the word or decorate it in any way they wish, cut it out and stick it onto the appropriate page of the book.

Extensions/variations
- Depending on the stages the children have reached, they can trace, copy or write whole words.
- Invite children to draw pictures and write more words or sentences to add to relevant pages of their choice.

Make a card

Learning objectives
- To create and write simple messages in meaningful contexts
- To talk about events that are to happen in the future and to describe to a familiar group the cards made for the occasions
- To handle materials, equipment and tools effectively, including pencils for writing
- To help children understand the importance of messages

What to do
- All sorts of celebrations will arise over the academic year – birthdays, name days, Mother's Day, Father's Day, religious festivals, etc. There is nothing more satisfying to children than to make a special greetings card for the occasion. They often learn to write 'love from' and their name without even thinking about it!
- Each child should be offered an attractive piece of card folded in half. It is helpful to buy good materials for the activity because the more attractive the card is, the more effort the children will put into their greetings. Help the children to decide on wording appropriate to the occasion.
- The children will have reached different stages in writing ability. Be prepared to scribe for some, to write words to be traced or copied for others and to support others as they compose and try to write and spell their own messages. Provide lots of encouragement to have a go at writing their words by themselves. If necessary, write an interpretation somewhere on the card.
- Encourage the children to think of good ways of illustrating their cards. This can be by drawing or cutting and sticking – glitter-sticking always goes down very well. While the children are doing this they are developing their skills of hand/eye coordination.

Topic
Celebrations

Resources
- Card
- Pens
- Pencils
- Crayons
- Paper
- Scissors
- Glue
- Stickers
- Craft materials

- All the time the children are engaged in this activity you should be talking them through it so that they are learning lots of language and vocabulary.

Extension/variation
- Invite the children to show their cards individually to the group, and describe them. Ask the group for comments – what do they like about each card?

Links to home
- Encourage the children to make cards at home to send to their friends at the group.

Multicultural link
- Be aware of different ethnic festivals that you can celebrate together and invite families of all cultures to share their cards and other customs and traditions with the group.

Related activity
- Send a letter (see page 163)

Have a go

Topic
Any topic

Resources
- Large sheet of paper
- Black felt-tipped pen
- Easel, white board or flip chart

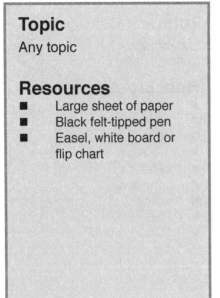

Learning objectives
- To use phonic knowledge to write simple regular words
- To use memory skills to write some common irregular words and names

Preparation
- Set up the flip chart, easel or whiteboard so that all the children can see it easily. Have an idea in your head for a story, shared event or personal experience you and the children can write about together. For example, you may have been on a trip to the shops or the park, which would be a good stimulus.

What to do
- Tell the children that you are all going to write your 'story' together, that you will do most of the writing but that you know they will be able to do some of it, too. Discuss what you are going to write about.
- Invite the children to think up a title, or heading, for the writing. When you have come to a consensus, ask if any of the children can write any of those words – they may feel able to try to write words such as 'the', 'at' or 'to', etc. Write some of the words yourself and encourage individual children out to write any of the words they are prepared to attempt. Some children may want to write certain letters but not whole words. Give lots of praise and encouragement for everyone's efforts.
- Make sure you point out the spaces that have to be left between words. Carry on in this way until the 'story' has been written.
- Read it back, all together.

Extension/variation
- Work with individual children in the same way, encouraging them to take over the writing whenever they feel able, so that you are writing together in an 'apprenticeship' manner (see page 123).

Design a cover

Learning objectives
- To write simple words and phrases to form book titles
- To experiment with colour, design and texture

Preparation
- Check the children's knowledge about what the cover of a book is. Have a look at the covers of some of the books that the children know well and discuss what the covers tell them.

What to do
- Read, or tell, a story to the children and talk about the story with them. Who are the important characters? What are the important events? What is the story called? – or can they think of something it might be called?
- Suggest to the children that, if they were going to make a book about the story, they would need to design a cover. Talk about what they might see on the cover of the book – encourage ideas and verbal descriptions.
- Ask the children to design their covers. Take suggestions from them for the title of the book and help them to write a title, using strategies such as phonic knowledge, experience of initial sounds and memory of common words. Support some children who may still need to use copy-writing or over-copying strategies in order to write recognizable letters.

Extensions/variations
- Ask each child to share their design with the group, describing it and giving reasons for their choices.
- Make a display of the book covers with a caption giving a short blurb about the book. Read the blurb with the children.

Related activities
- Copy-writing (see page 132)
- Over-copying (see page 131)

Topic
Any topic

Resources
- Paper or card
- Pencils
- Crayons
- Felt-tipped pens
- Known storybooks

Easy peasy book

Topic

Any topic

Resources
- Paper
- Card
- Hole punch
- Scissors
- String

Learning objectives
- To know that information can be relayed in the form of print and pictures
- To use reading writing and drawing skills and phonic knowledge to make a simple book

Preparation
- The preparation is whatever activity you have been working on with the children. Invite children to draw and write about a recent activity, outing or game that they have been working on.

What to do
- Help with tracing, copying and emergent writing where necessary. Scribe words that children ask you to write for them, or specifically ask them to compose and dictate words to you. Make sure their individual names are on their pieces of work.
- Take two pieces of card for the book's 'covers' and punch a hole through the top left-hand corner. Assemble the pages.

Punch a hole straight through the top left-hand corner.
- Put the pages inside the covers, give the front cover a title and the group's name as author and illustrator. Hang the book where the children can reach it easily, to read and share. The book will lie flat and will be easy to open.

Extensions/variations
- Give the children plenty of opportunity to share the book with each other.
- You can make books specific to any of the key areas by choosing to use particular activities as the content.

Links to home
- Encourage the children to take turns to take the book home to share it with their parents.

A simple flap book

Learning objectives
- To know that information and stories can be relayed in the forms of print and pictures
- To use reading, writing and drawing skills to make a simple book
- To attempt to write words, labels, captions and short sentences to communicate meaning
- To handle and manipulate materials and tools effectively

Preparation

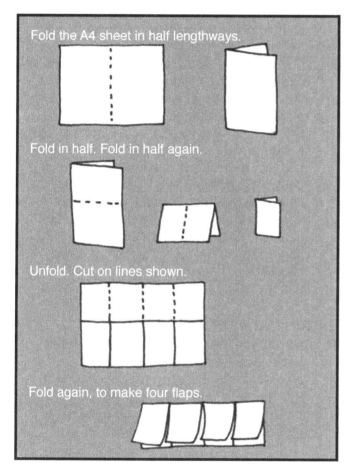

Fold the A4 sheet in half lengthways.

Fold in half. Fold in half again.

Unfold. Cut on lines shown.

Fold again, to make four flaps.

Topic
Any topic

Resources
- A4 sheet for each child
- Felt-tipped pens
- Scissors
- Sticky tape

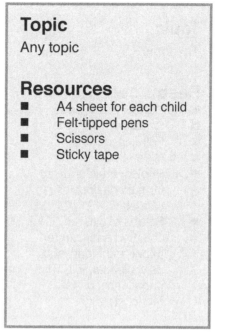

What to do
- Support each child in folding her sheet of paper, as shown in the diagram. Show her how the flaps work and explain that together you can make the paper into a book. Discuss a topic for the four pages and encourage the child to decide on a sentence or question for each flap and a relevant illustration and reply for each page underneath. Help and support her to achieve these by drawing the pictures and writing, copying or tracing the words.
- For example on page 1 you might want: *What colour is the crocodile?* Then, under the flap draw a crocodile, colour it red and write: *The crocodile is red.*
- Continue your chosen theme for the four pages and flaps. Join the folded edges together with sticky tape.
- Write the title and the child's name (author) on the cover page.
- Read through the book together.

Extensions/variations
- Make a collection of individual flap books.
- Make a larger flap book with the whole group, using two sheets of A3 and joining the two lots of flaps together after they are illustrated and the text is written.

More flap books

Topic
Any topic

Resources
- Card or sugar paper
- Scissors
- Felt-tipped pens
- Glue-stick
- Photos or pictures cut from magazines or catalogues
- Scraps of different coloured and textured paper and fabric, such as wallpaper, foil, shiny paper, lace, curtain fabric, etc

Learning objectives
- To know that information and stories can be relayed in the form of print and pictures
- To attempt to write words, labels, captions and short sentences to communicate meaning
- To handle and manipulate materials and tools effectively

Preparation
- Make small books with the card or sugar paper by folding, stapling or tying it, whichever is the most appropriate. You don't need too many pages.

What to do
- Ask the child what she would like her book to be about and help her to find some appropriate pictures. You will need half as many pictures as you have pages.
- Help the child to glue her first chosen picture/photo on the first right-hand inside page. Talk about what she could write about it and help her to compose a caption or sentence on the left-hand side. Use writing

techniques appropriate to her level to help her write, or scribe the composed words.
- Invite the child to choose a piece of fabric or paper and cut it to cover the picture. Show the child how to glue it into place at the top of the picture, so that it provides a flap.
- Continue until all the pages are completed.
- Encourage the child to make up a title for her flap book and to create the front cover design. Read through the book with the child, helping her to 'read' the words first and then looking under the flap to see the surprise. This will help her to understand the connection between words and pictures, and she will never tire of saying, 'I wonder what's under the flap…' even though she knows!

Extensions/variations
- Encourage the children to share their flap books with each other.
- Try to arrange a special sharing time with their parents, perhaps when they collect the children, when all the children and all the parents look at the books together.

Links to home
- Send books home for sharing.
- Encourage children and parents to make books at home and bring them in to share with the group.

Simple pop-up books

Learning objectives
- To create a character for a story and to write about it, using words, labels, captions or short sentences
- To manipulate materials and tools effectively and explore new techniques of design and function
- To create simple representations of people and use original ideas in design and technology, art and stories

Preparation
- Fold each sheet of paper in half width ways. Turn down a small triangle from the fold and press it down, then straighten it up again and turn it down against the other side of the folded paper and press. Open the sheet of paper and push the triangle inside, then fold again and press.
- When you open the page, the triangle will pop up.

What to do
- Give the children small pieces of paper and invite them to draw and colour characters. Talk with each child about who her character might be and whether it is someone she knows, someone from a book, or someone made up.
- Support the children as they fold the pictures down the centre so that the blank side of the paper is on the inside and then cut the characters out. If any of them are too small or complicated, suggest to the children that they just cut an oval or rectangular shape around them instead.
- Carefully matching the folded lines, stick the characters on to the folded-down triangles so that the characters are *inside* the pages and, when you open the pages, they pop up.
- The children now need to compose some text about their page and their character, which you can scribe or help them to write using early or emergent writing strategies.
- Stick the pages back to back to make a book, and give it a cover.

Topic
Any topic

Resources
- Paper
- Pencils
- Felt-tipped pens
- Scissors
- Glue-sticks
- Card

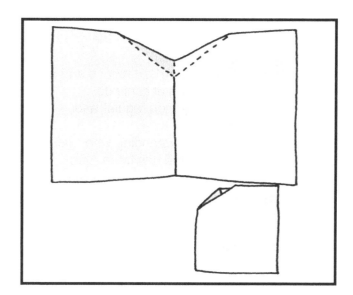

Extension/variation
- It might be quite difficult, on the first attempt, to bring all of the characters into a consistent storyline but, once the children have the idea of how the pop-up works, suggest you make up a story first together and then create the characters to fit it.

Photo albums

Topic
Any topic

Resources
- Camera
- An occasion to photograph
- Card or sugar paper
- Felt-tipped pens
- Glue
- Ring clips

Learning objectives
- To record a significant event in the group's life
- To attempt to write words, captions and short sentences in meaningful contexts
- To learn to read common regular and irregular words
- To demonstrate understanding when talking with others about what has been read

Preparation
- Choose an event of some importance to the group, for example, a trip, a walk, a visit, a party, etc. Take lots of photographs of the children and the things that interest them.

What to do
- To assemble the book you will need to have pictures on the left-hand page and text on the right-hand page.
- With small groups of children at a time, stick one photograph to each left-hand page. For the right-hand page, ask the children what they would like to say about the photo and demonstrate model writing simple text. Encourage and support children as they

choose to trace or copy the writing and to add words and sentences of their own.
- Decide on a title. Make the front and back covers out of card, write the title and give an authorship.
- With the children's help, assemble the pages in order, taking care of the sequence. Number the pages.
- Punch holes and secure with ring clips.

Extensions/variations
- Share the book often with the children, inviting them to discuss the pictures and 'read' the accompanying text with you, with support.
- Make the book available for 'reading' times and encourage the children to read it together.

Links to home
- Give the children opportunities to take the book home.

© Irene Yates
www.brilliantpublications.co.uk

Family album

Learning objectives
● To write names, words, labels, captions and sentences in meaninful contexts
● To understand that non-fiction books contain information
● To know and talk about similarities and differences among families

Preparation
● Make up a set of little books, one for each child. If you use three sheets of folded A4 paper, for each book, it will contain 8 usable pages plus the inside of the front and back covers.

What to do
● Talk about families. Ask the children to suggest what a family is and who might belong to a family. Be sensitive towards children who feel they haven't got a family and explain, simply, that their family might be the people that they live with. Discuss the fact that there are all kinds of families, that everyone's family is different and that people don't have to be the same as each other.
● Encourage the children to use relationship words – *mother, father, grandmother, grandfather, brother, sister, aunt, uncle, cousin.*
● Help the children to write *My Family* as their title, or *Who is this?,* if they prefer to. Ask each child to write their name on the cover as the author.
● Inside the book, ask the children to draw a picture on each page representing someone in their family and help them to write who it is –*my granddad, my nan, my cousin.*

Topic
Families

Resources
■ Paper
■ Card
■ Pencils
■ Felt-tipped pens
■ Stapler

(1–5)

Encourage them to be as imaginative as possible – they might, for instance, put their favourite toy on the last page.

Extensions/variations
● Be sensitive to children with unconventional families. If there are difficulties, ask the children to make up a family, which needn't be 'real' – it could be an animal family or a toy family.
● Extend the writing by encouraging a sentence for each member of the family, eg *This is my dad cooking the dinner.*

Links to home
● Send the books home for the parents to share with the children.

Zig-zag book

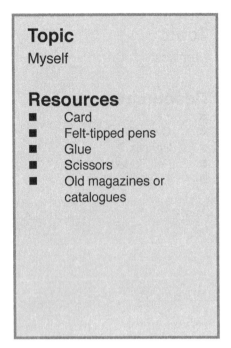

Topic

Myself

Resources
- Card
- Felt-tipped pens
- Glue
- Scissors
- Old magazines or catalogues

What to do
- Discuss the concept of the book with the children. A zig-zag book can stand up along a shelf. It has pictures and/or text on both sides.
- Talk about what the book will be about – eg numbers, colours, pets, family, etc.
- Decide with the children which will be the first and, therefore, the title page – leave this until last.
- Support the children as they illustrate their pages, by drawing pictures or cutting them out and sticking them into place, then write the text for their book. Number the pages with the children, making sure they understand you don't number the title page (cover). When you get to the end of one side of the zig-zag, turn it over and carry on numbering.
- Decide on the title and demonstrate writing it and the authors' names.
- Read through the book together. Display it prominently.

Learning objective
- To design the pages of a book, sticking to a main theme and making pictures to accompany a simple text of words, labels or captions

Extensions/variations
- Help children to make individual books appropriate to their own lives and experiences.
- Encourage the children to use whatever writing techniques are appropriate for their stage of development.

Preparation
- Fold the pieces of card to make a zig-zag; the number of 'pages' will depend upon the length of your card.

Going for a walk book

Learning objectives
- To design the pages of a book, sticking to a main theme, drawing pictures and writing a text of simple sentences to accompany them
- To handle materials and tools effectively, including pencils for writing

Preparation
- Talk to all the children about making a 'going for a walk' book before working with them individually. Make a simple book for each child, with three or four pages.

What to do
- Ask the child to draw a small picture of herself on a piece of card, to cut it out and to stick it to one end of a piece of string or ribbon with sticky tape.
- Make up the story of the walk. It might be a walk to the park or the shops. Invite the child to make up a sentence for each page and scribe it for her, encouraging her to trace or copy the words, or support her as she writes the words for herself. Encourage her to illustrate each page.
- Work on the cover together and support the child as she chooses a title and writes her name as the author.
- Make a small pocket with card and tape it to the front cover. Tape the other end of the string or ribbon into this pocket and then place the cut-out child into the pocket.
- When she opens her book to read the story, the child can slip the cut-out picture of herself out of the pocket and 'walk' it along with the story.

Extensions/variations
- If the children are able, let them make the books themselves, using A4 sheets as pages and just help them to put them together.
- Read *Rosie's Walk* with the children.
- Make a 'going for a walk' book based on the story of *Rosie's Walk*.
- Keep all of the books easily accessible for reading and sharing.

Topic
Gardening/environment

Resources
- Card
- Hole punch
- Felt-tipped pens
- Paper
- Scissors
- Glue
- Sticky tape
- Pencils
- Crayons
- Ribbon or string
- *Rosie's Walk* by Pat Hutchins (Bodley Head)

Treasure map

Topic

Water

Resources
- Pirate activities
- Large sheets of paper
- Pens or crayons
- A simple map to show children how a map works

Learning objectives
- To give meaning to marks while drawing and writing
- To attempt to write words, labels and simple sentences to communicate meaning
- To handle writing and drawing tools effectively
- To represent ideas through art and role-play

Preparation
- Have pirate role-play activities available.

What to do
- Show the children your map and ask if they know what it is. Talk with them about whether they have ever seen other maps, when adults might use maps and what they are for.
- Suggest that if the pirates wish to find the buried treasure on the island they need a map of where the treasure is. Ask the children if they could make maps for the pirates to use.

- Talk them through making their maps – they need to draw the shoreline of the island, perhaps draw a tree, put in anything else they think is important to show the pirates where to go, put a cross where the treasure is and 'write' on their map, 'The treasure is here'.
- Be happy to accept whatever marks they want to make. If they want you to help by writing certain letters or words, you can scribe for them. Some children may want you to write words or make symbols for them to copy or trace over.

Extensions/variations
- Colour the maps.
- Make maps of your own setting.

Related activities
- Be a pirate (see page 53)
- Message in a bottle (see page 157)

Message in a bottle

Learning objective
● To make marks or begin to write letters, words or simple sentences to communicate meaning, for different purposes

Preparation
● Look for opportunities for the children to role-play being pirates.

What to do
● Explain to the children how pirates trapped on an island might be desperate to send somebody a message so that they could rescue them. Discuss how the pirates could send the message, if they had no computers or e-mail, no post boxes, no phones or mobiles and nobody calling at the island to take a message for them.
● Suggest that the pirates could put a message in a bottle and throw it into the sea. The sea would wash the bottle away and send it to another land where someone would find it and be able to rescue them.
● Ask the children to suggest what the message might say.
● Help the children to each 'write' a message. Allow them to do this independently and don't force children to identify sounds or write letters and words unless they are ready to do so. Some may only be able to make a scrawl across a page. Respond positively to all of the children's attempts at writing and ask them to read to you what they have made their messages say. Put the messages into the bottle, seal it and let them 'cast it into the sea' (or at least roll it across the floor!) from the island.

Extensions/variations
● Line up an adult with a different group of children to receive the messages and organize a rescue party.
● In circle time, have the children, in role, recount their experiences and show their messages.

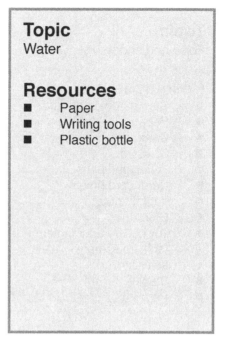

Topic
Water

Resources
■ Paper
■ Writing tools
■ Plastic bottle

Related activities
● Be a pirate (see page 53)
● Treasure map (see page 156)

Make a restaurant

3–4

Topic
Food and shopping

Resources
- Corrugated cardboard
- Paper
- Card
- Scissors
- Felt-tipped pens
- Cardboard boxes
- Yoghurt pots
- Glue
- Toy cutlery and canteen/table equipment if available
- Stapler
- Pencils

© Irene Yates

Learning objectives
- To attempt to write lists of food words and prices and to take note of food orders and numbers of customers
- To discuss and answer questions about experiences
- To represent their own thoughts and ideas through role-play

Preparation
- Talk to the children about how a restaurant works, what it's for, where the children have been and what different kinds of restaurants there are.

What to do
- You need cardboard boxes, turned upside-down to be tables, and cardboard boxes with no top and one of the four sides cut away, to be chairs. Set up as many tables and chairs as your restaurant will take.
- Make plates and cutlery out of card. Place a yoghurt pot in the centre of each table with some cut-out and coloured card flowers in.
- Help children to make a group menu on a large piece of card or a board and stand it against a wall. Encourage them to make

small menus to put on the tables. Invite the children to suggest items that might appear on the menus and support them in using phonic knowledge to attempt to write them down, giving clues or scribing where necessary.
- Help the children to decide who will be guests and who will be waiters to start the play. Equip the waiters with notebooks (make them out of small pieces of paper stapled together) and pencils to take the orders.
- If space and imagination permit, make cookers for one or two chefs and make pans and food out of card.
- Suggest that the children who are visiting the restaurant might like to dress up to go out for their meal.

Extensions/variations
- Make a fast food restaurant.
- Give the children lots of opportunities for talking about what they have been doing and playing.
- Make some real food and drinks to serve at the restaurant.

Links to home
- Invite parents to visit the restaurant.

Related activity
- Set up a fish and chip shop (see page 159)

Set up a fish and chip shop Writing

Learning objectives
- To attempt to write labels and captions and to communicate meaning
- To discuss and answer questions about experiences
- To introduce a narrative and represent their own ideas through role-play

Preparation
- Talk about the local fish and chip shop. Encourage the children to tell you about it. Suggest making a fish and chip shop in the role-play area.

What to do
- With the children's help, make the fish and chip shop. Make a counter from a cardboard box or table. Have two big cardboard boxes as friers, one to cook the fish in, one to cook the chips in. Make a microwave oven by cutting the front of a box so that it opens. Cut out a 'window' and cover it with cling film or cellophane. Ask the children to make switches and dials to stick onto the microwave.
- Make the fish, chips and other food items out of card – you will need lots!
- Ask the children to suggest notices, labels and signs you will need:
  - Open/Closed
  - Frying now
  - Fish and chips
  - Pies and burgers
  - A price list.
- Write them with the children dictating to you, so that they can see the writing process in action. Encourage the children to 'write' their own labels, too.

Topic
Food and shopping

Resources
- Cardboard boxes
- Scissors
- Cling film or cellophane
- Coloured paper
- Card (lots)
- Glue
- Till
- Paper hats
- Aprons
- Plastic utensils
- Paper for wrapping

Extensions/variations
- Make the fish and chip shop a part of everyday play.
- Set up a burger bar or a pizzeria in the same way.
- Give the children opportunities to talk about their experiences.

Related activities
- Fish and chips (see page 67)
- Make a restaurant (see page 158)

Wild animal park

Topic
Animals

Resources
- Soft toys
- Paper
- Card
- Scissors
- Felt-tipped pens
- Cardboard boxes
- String
- Silvery foil
- Cling film or cellophane
- Dowel or stick
- Reference books about animals
- Lots of space

Learning objectives
- To use phonic knowledge to write labels and captions
- To write signs with real purpose during imaginative role-play
- To play cooperatively within a group to develop and act out narratives in role-play

Preparation
- Discuss the idea of a 'wild animal park' and invite the children to tell you about any wild animal park or zoo experiences they have had, what they think a wild animal park is for and what kind of animals they might see there.
- Ask the children to bring in any animal toys they might like to lend to the group's wild animal park (make sure they are labelled clearly with owners' names).

What to do
- Ask the children to sort the toys into sets – elephants, lions, monkeys, seals, etc. Make a habitat for each set, using cardboard boxes for sleeping quarters or pens. If you are short of certain species, draw them on card, colour them and cut them out.
- Make fish out of card and stick silvery scales to them. Cut out the sides of a box and fill in the spaces with cling film or cellophane to make an aquarium. Suspend the fish with cotton from a stick or dowel across the box.
- Make labels and captions for each set of animals, for example:
  - Do not feed the monkeys!
  - Don't poke the lion!
  - Come back to feed the seals at 3 o'clock!
- Make entrance tickets for the children to sell and buy.
- Make a display of reference books for the children to search for information.

Extensions/variations
- Make a 'Wild Animal Park' book.
- Record the children telling stories about the wild animals or acting out narratives. Encourage them to include lots of animal noises and sound effects. Allow them to play back the recordings and listen to their own voices.
- Take lots of photos so that you can discuss the project with the children when it has finished.
- Give the children opportunities to address the group, talking about what they have done.
- Provide opportunities for children to listen to CDs and watch DVDs containing stories or facts about wild animals and the sounds they make.

Links to home
- Invite parents to visit your wild animal park.

© Irene Yates
www.brilliantpublications.co.uk

Transport

Learning objectives
- To use language to imagine and recreate roles and experiences
- To attempt to write labels, captions, names, words and short sentences to communicate meaning
- To play cooperatively to act out narratives and represent thoughts and feelings through role-play

Preparation
- Discuss various modes of travel and invite the children to tell you their experiences of the different kinds of transport they have come into contact with.

What to do
- Choose a mode of transport that the children seem to be fairly enthusiastic about. Use as many cardboard boxes as you have available to become that kind of transport.
- Support the children as they add wheels and other decorations to cardboard boxes to create cars. Make a petrol station out of boxes, furniture or recycled materials and issue receipts for petrol. Make driving licences and tax and insurance papers for the drivers.
- A little imagination can turn the cars into aeroplanes and the petrol station into an airport. Make passports and travel documents and invite the travellers to write postcards to send home.
- When these modes of transport have been exhausted make boats. Again, make passports and travel documents, fishing rights licences, ships' diaries, captains' notes, etc.

Extensions/variations
- Give lots of opportunities for the children to recount both their real life and their imagined experiences.
- Cut up travel brochures to make maps and information books about places to stay.
- 'Read' maps and atlases with the children.

Topic
Transport and travel

Resources
- Corrugated cardboard
- Paper
- Card
- Scissors
- Felt-tipped pens
- Cardboard boxes

Write me a letter

Topic
People who help us

Resources
- Paper
- Black felt-tipped pen

Learning objectives
- To attempt to write words and sentences in meaningful contexts, to suit different purposes
- To begin to read and understand simple sentences and to demonstrate understanding of what has been read

Preparation
- If possible, set up a play situation where a natural outcome would be for a letter to be written, for example someone in hospital, someone on a visit, someone on holiday.

What to do
- Suggest to the child that she writes a letter appropriate to the situation. For example, if someone is in hospital she might write to ask how they are and send her best wishes and promise to go and see them. Suggest that she makes up the letter, tells you what it needs to say and that you write down the words with her or support her as she does it for herself.

- Prompt the child gently and give her plenty of time to verbalize her thoughts and get them into the right order – she will be practising the skills of composition, staying on task and sequencing, as well as observing you using appropriate punctuation and grammar as her message is recorded.
- Encourage the child to write her own name and any other words she can write at the end of the letter.
- Read it back carefully, with the child, pointing to the words as you go and encourage the child to read it back again to you.

Extension/variation
- Use this dictation technique to write:
  - stories
  - shopping lists
  - stories about events in the children's lives.

Related activity
- Send an e-mail (see page 122)
- Send a letter (see page 163)

Send a letter

Learning objectives
- To attempt to write names, simple words and short sentences, using memory and phonic knowledge
- To know that print carries meaning and, in English, is read from left to right and top to bottom

Preparation
- Talk with the children about letters, how they get from one place to another, and what you do when you've written one, to check their knowledge.

What to do
- Suggest to the children that you make a class or group post box. Show them the cardboard box and ask them how you can make it into a post box. Explain that the post box will need somewhere for the letters to go in when they are posted, and somewhere for the letters to come out when they are collected.
- Cut a slot in the front for the letters to go in, and make a 'door' at the back for collecting the post. Secure the door with a piece of sticky tape.
- Ask the children to help you decide on the collection times and make a label for the front of the post box and glue it on.
- Invite the children to write their letters and cards to each other. Help where necessary by supporting emerging writing or scribing for some children to copy or trace over letters and words. Make sure that everybody has at least one letter to receive.
- Post the letters.

Topic
People who help us

Resources
- Large cardboard box
- Scissors
- Sticky tape
- Paper
- Glue
- Felt-tipped pens
- Writing paper or card
- Pencils

Extensions/variations
- Give the children turns to collect, sort and deliver the post.
- Write a 'real' letter to the group and take the children to post it.

Links to home
- Invite the children to write letters to their families.

Related activities
- Post delivery person (see page 84)
- Send an e-mail (see page 122)
- Write me a letter (see page 162)

Taking messages

Topic
People who help us

Resources
- Old phones, mobiles, pretend phones, etc
- Note pads
- Self-stick notes
- Pencils

Learning objectives
- To use phonic knowledge to write words in ways that match their spoken sounds
- To write simple messages and to understand when and why these might be useful or necessary
- To respond to instructions involving several ideas and to answer 'how' and 'why' questions

Preparation
- Invite the children into a role-play situation with you where one of you needs to give a message and the other one needs to write it down.

What to do
- Talk about message-taking situations. The children may have lots that they can think of – or may not have seen and heard anyone taking messages. The more situations you can imagine with the children, the better, because you will be feeding in lots of new vocabulary and language.
- For example, you might be telephoning the doctor or the dentist to make an

appointment, or telephoning the florist to arrange for some flowers to be delivered, or telephoning home to remind someone to record your favourite television programme. Make the story as interesting as you can.
- Decide which of you is going to take the message and which is going to give it. Have a clear message worked out between you to begin with.
- Encourage the children to 'write' the message in any way they can. Read the message back together.

Extensions/variations
- During a group or circle time, invite children to talk about what they have been doing in their message-taking games and show each other their messages.
- Encourage the children to learn how to give their name and address clearly on the phone, and how to ring emergency services.

Related activity
- Make a call (see page 21)

Making labels

Learning objectives
● To create labels and captions, using a computer
● To select and use technology for a particular purpose

What to do
● Suggest to the children that you could put labels on some of the equipment in the rooms and the outoor area of the setting. Suggest that you could make them together, using the computer.
● Decide on your labels. You might want to just print 'crayons', for example, or you might want to write something like 'Be gentle with the guinea pig'.
● Choose a large, clear font that the children can discriminate easily.
● Ask them, 'Which sound comes first? So that is the letter ….' Talk them though the whole activity. Help the children to type the letters in by showing them how to locate them on the keyboard.
● Help the children to save and print.
● Cut out the labels and stick them where the children want them to be.

Extensions/variations
● You can make this quite a regular activity because labels and captions tend to get tatty very quickly. Help the children to see that, if you tidy them up by making new ones every so often, you keep your base nice and tidy.
● Be prepared to change the wording if someone comes up with a better idea. Again, make new labels.

Links to home
● Make labels for the children to take home, eg 'Mia's bedroom', 'Atak's rabbit'.

Topic
Any topic

Resources
■ Computer
■ Word processing program
■ Printer
■ Paper or thin card (white or light colours)
■ Scissors
■ Reusable mastic adhesive

What's your favourite?

Topic
Any topic

Resources
- Computer
- Word-processing program
- Printer
- Paper
- Nursery rhymes (see pages 177–182)
- Computer gallery of pictures (optional)

Learning objectives
- To understand how to write down the words of a well-known rhyme in order to read and say it together
- To write simple sentences that can be read by children and adults
- To find letters on a keyboard, to understand how to make spaces and to begin to type separate words
- To begin to use a computer to type in, check, save and print out a rhyme

What to do
- Suggest to the children that you make a printed copy of one of their favourite rhymes. Give plenty of time and discussion to choosing a rhyme that all the group want to reproduce.
- Type in the rhyme, inviting the children to help as much as possible. For example, they may be able to help you type in the title. Choose a large, clear font with letters that the children can discriminate.

- When it is all typed in, ask the children to help you to 'read' it back, to make sure there are no mistakes. Read the rhyme with the children, pointing to the words. Show the children how to 'save'.
- With the children's help, print out the rhyme, encouraging them to move the mouse and click the button to carry out the task with your support.
- Read the printed rhyme together.

Extensions/variations
- If you have the facility, illustrate the rhyme with pictures from the computer gallery, or invite each group of children to draw pictures to illustrate their rhyme.
- Print a different rhyme for each group of children and put them together to make a book.

Keeping a writing record

Learning objectives
- To give meaning to marks while drawing and writing
- To handle equipment and tools effectively
- To use some clearly identifiable letters to communicate meaning
- To use phonic knowledge to write words that match spoken sounds
- To attempt to write short sentences in meaningful contexts

Preparation
- Make a notebook for each child, showing their name clearly. Keep them where they are accessible to the children so that they can do some 'writing' at any time of the session. Encourage them to be independent in this aspect.

Topic
Any topic

Resources
- A small notebook for each child
- Pencils
- Felt-tipped pens
- Crayons
- Writing tools always available
- Tape recorder
- Blank cassette tape

What to do
- Explain to the children that the notebooks are for them to record their ideas, messages and stories in. Show them which is the right-hand page of each double-page spread. The right-hand side is *their* side, the left-hand side is *your* side.
- Encourage them to write messages, stories, etc, whenever they want to, on the right-hand page, and perhaps draw a picture underneath the message, to illustrate it.
- On the left-hand page, write the date the message was written, decode the message (with the child's help) and record any information you feel is important, such as comments on any skill development or ideas for future teaching.
- At the end of the term or year you will have a see-at-a-glance record of the child's writing development.

Extensions/variations
- The children do not need to 'read' every scribble story to you for you to write the interpretation – you could ask them to 'read' some of their messages into a tape recorder instead.
- Give suggestions for stories or messages they might write in their books from work you are doing in other areas of learning.

Rhyming pairs template

**Communication and Language
with Literacy**

Jigsaw template

Order, order template

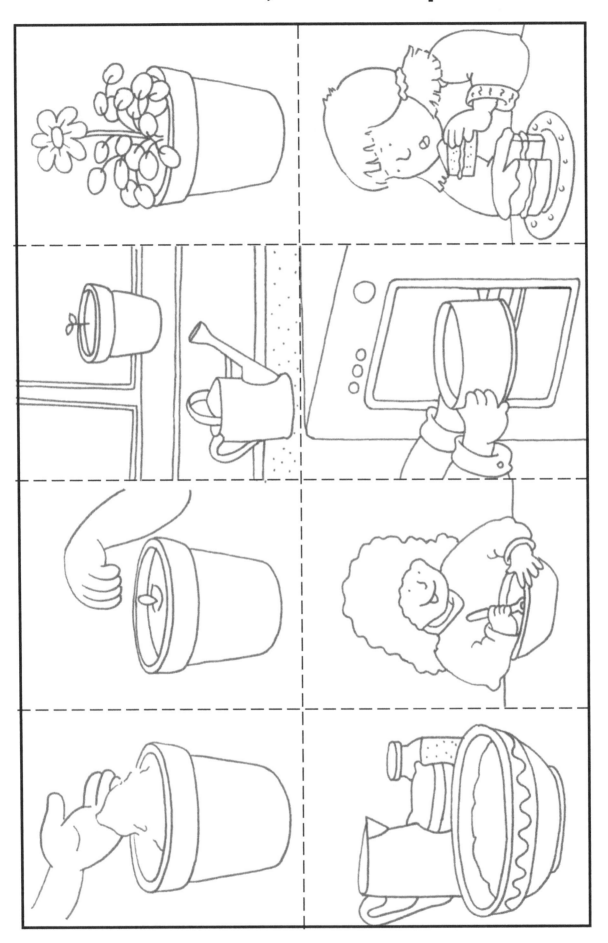

Communication and Language with Literacy

© Irene Yates
www.brilliantpublications.co.uk

Same and different template

Letter train template

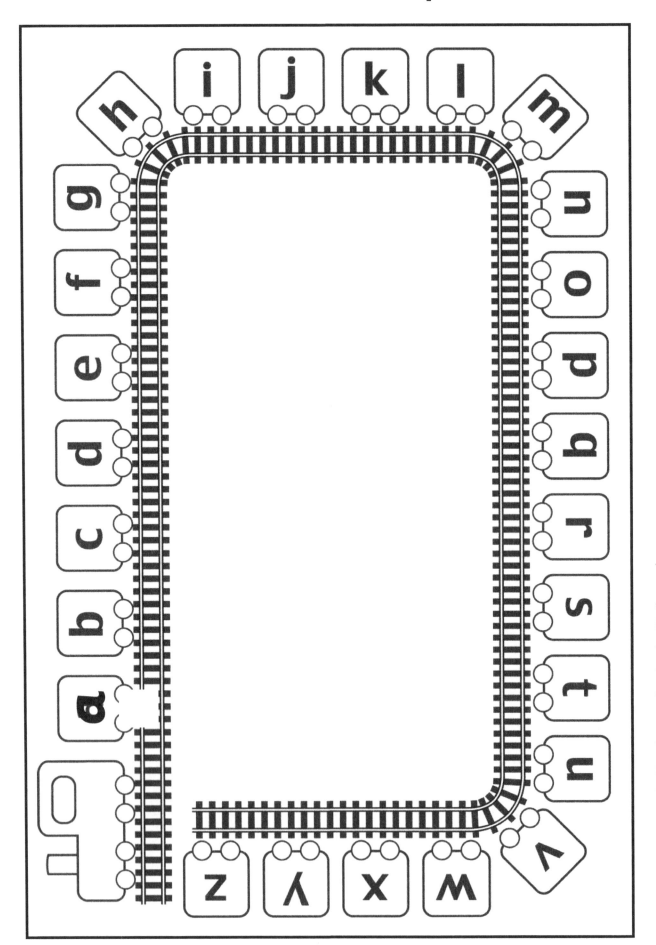

**Communication and Language
with Literacy**

© Irene Yates
www.brilliantpublications.co.uk

Match the letter template, 1

a b c

d e f

g h i

Match the letter template, 2

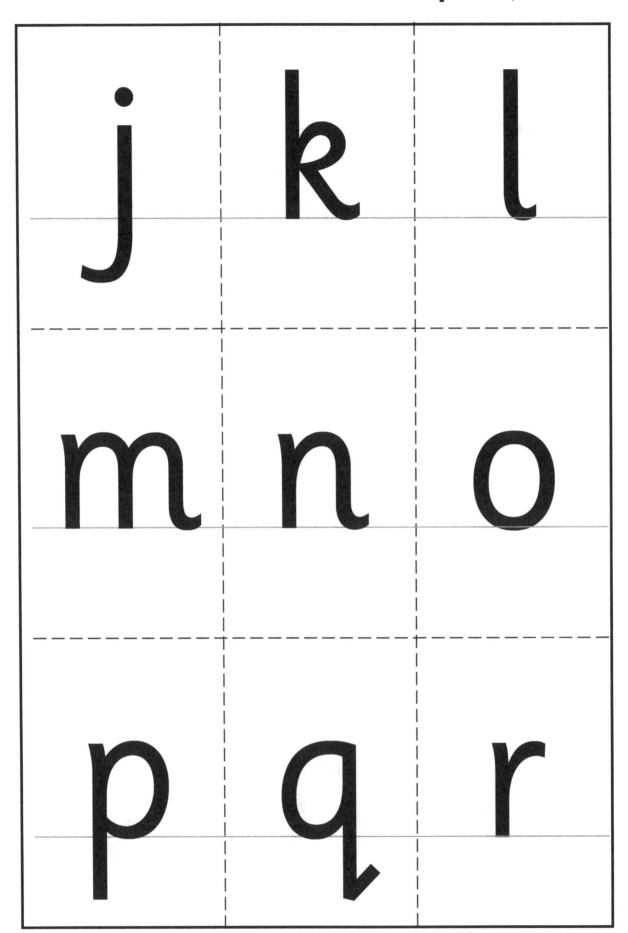

**Communication and Language
with Literacy**

Match the letter template, 3

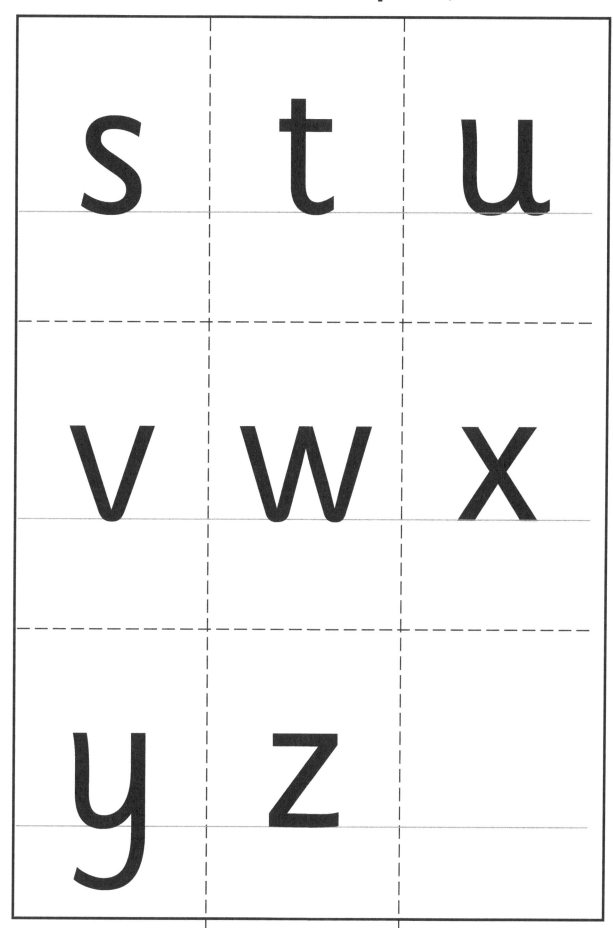

**Communication and Language
with Literacy**

Forming letters

a b c d e f g h i j k l m n
o p q r s t u v w x y z

a b c d e f g h i j k l m n
o p q r s t u v w x y z

**Communication and Language
with Literacy**

© Irene Yates
www.brilliantpublications.co.uk

Rhymes

Action rhymes

Here is the church
Here is the church	(*touch fists at knuckles*)
And here is the steeple,	(*open fists and touch fingertips*)
Open the doors	(*open hands wide*)
And see all the people.	(*wriggle fingers*)
Here is the vicar going upstairs	(*walk fingers upwards*)
And here he is, a-saying his prayers.	(*hands together for prayer*)

Incy Wincy spider
Incy Wincy spider	
Climbed up the water spout.	(*fingers climbing into air*)
Down came the rain and	
Washed the spider out.	(*flutter fingers down*)
Out came the sunshine and	
Dried up all the rain,	(*stretch hands out for sunshine*)
So Incy Wincy spider	
Climbed up the spout again!	(*fingers climb high into air*)

I hear thunder, I hear thunder
I hear thunder, I hear thunder,	
Hark, don't you? Hark, don't you?	(*hands to ears, listening*)
Pitter patter raindrops,	
pitter patter raindrops,	(*hands fluttering down as rain*)
I'm wet through! So are you!	

Two little dickie birds
Two little dickie birds	
Sitting on a wall	(*make beak shapes with each hand, by putting thumb and forefinger together*)
One named Peter, one named Paul.	(*open each beak in turn*)
Fly away, Peter! Fly away, Paul!	(*flutter each hand behind back*)
Come back, Peter! Come back, Paul!	(*flutter each hand back*)

The wheels on the bus go round and round

The wheels on the bus go round and round,
(hands rolling round each other)
Round and round, round and round,
(repeat movement)
The wheels on the bus go round and round,
(repeat movement)
All day long.

The driver on the bus goes, 'Sit down, please,
(wagging finger)
Sit down, please, sit down, please'
(repeat movement)
The driver on the bus goes, 'Sit down, please,'
(repeat movement)
All day long.

The old men on the bus go nod, nod, nod,
(nodding, tiredness)
Nod, nod, nod, nod, nod, nod,
(repeat movement)
The old men on the bus go nod, nod, nod,
(repeat movement)
All day long.

The ladies on the bus go chitter, chatter, chitter
(chattering movements)
Chitter, chatter, chitter, chitter, chatter, chitter
(repeat movement)
The ladies on the bus go chitter, chatter, chitter
(repeat movement)
All day long.

The horn on the bus goes honk, honk, honk,
(thumb and fingers together)
Honk, honk, honk, honk, honk, honk,
(repeat movement)
The horn on the bus goes honk, honk, honk,
(repeat movement)
All day long.

The babies on the bus go wah, wah, wah,
(exaggerated crying expressions)
Wah, wah, wah, wah, wah, wah,
(repeat movement)
The babies on the bus go wah, wah, wah,
(repeat movement)
All day long.

Tommy Thumb

Tommy Thumb, Tommy Thumb, where are you?
Here I am, here I am,
(wriggle thumbs)
How do you do?

Peter Pointer, Peter Pointer, where are you?
Here I am, here I am,
(wriggle first fingers)
How do you do?

Toby Tall, Toby Tall, where are you?
Here I am, here I am,
(wriggle middle fingers)
How do you do?

Ruby Ring, Ruby Ring, where are you?
Here I am, here I am,
(wriggle third fingers)
How do you do?

Baby Small, Baby Small, where are you?
Here I am, here I am,
(put up little fingers)
How do you do?

Fingers all, fingers all where are you?
Here we are, here we are
(wriggle all fingers)
How do you do?

(get the children to hide their fists behind their backs and bring them out with their thumbs and fingers extended for each verse.)

Communication and Language with Literacy

© Irene Yates
www.brilliantpublications.co.uk

Marching rhyme

The grand old Duke of York

The grand old Duke of York
He had ten thousand men,
He marched them up to the top of the hill
And he marched them down again.
And when they were up, they were up.
And when they were down, they were
down.
And when they were only halfway up
They were neither up nor down!

Clapping rhymes

Rain, rain, go away

Rain, rain, go away,
Come again another day.
Rain, rain, go away,
Come again another day.

Pat-a-cake, pat-a-cake

Pat-a-cake, pat-a-cake,
Baker's man,
Bake me a cake as fast as you can.
Pit it and pat it and mark it with (*child's initial*),
Put it in the oven for (*child's name*) and me!

Hot cross buns!

Hot cross buns! Hot cross buns!
One a penny, two a penny, hot cross buns!
If you have no daughters, give them to
your sons,
One a penny, two a penny, hot cross buns!

If you're happy and you know it

If you're happy and you know it, clap your
hands,
(*clap, clap*)
If you're happy and you know it, clap your
hands,
(*clap, clap*)
If you're happy and you know it, and you
really want to show it,
If you're happy and you know it, clap your
hands.
(*clap, clap*)

(Substitute other actions and sounds, eg
'nod your head', 'say boo', etc.)

© Irene Yates
www.brilliantpublications.co.uk

Rhymes to learn and recite

Little Boy Blue

Little Boy Blue
Come blow your horn,
The sheep's in the meadow,
The cow's in the corn.
Where is the boy
Who looks after the sheep?
He's under a haystack
Fast asleep.
Will you wake him?
No, not I,
For if I do
He's sure to cry.

Three blind mice

Three blind mice,
Three blind mice,
See how they run!
See how they run!
They all ran after the farmer's wife,
Who cut off their tails with a carving knife,
Did you ever see such a thing in your life
As three blind mice?

See-saw, Margery Daw

See-saw, Margery Daw,
Johnny will have a new master.
He shall pay but a penny a day,
because he can't work any faster.

Hickory, dickory, dock

Hickory, dickory, dock,
The mouse ran up the clock,
The clock struck one,
The mouse ran down,
Hickory, dickory, dock.

One, two, buckle my shoe

One, two, buckle my shoe;
Three, four, knock at the door;
Five, six, pick up sticks;
Seven, eight, lay them straight;
Nine, ten, my fat hen,
Eleven, twelve, dig and delve;
Thirteen, fourteen, maids a-courting;
Fifteen, sixteen, maids in the kitchen,
Seventeen, eighteen, maids in waiting;
Nineteen, twenty, my plate's empty.

There was a crooked man

There was a crooked man
And he walked a crooked mile,
He found a crooked sixpence
Upon a crooked stile;
He bought a crooked cat,
Which caught a crooked mouse,
And they all lived together
In a little crooked house.

Doctor Foster went to Gloucester

Doctor Foster went to Gloucester
In a shower of rain.
He stepped in a puddle
Right up to his middle
And never went there again!

**Communication and Language
with Literacy**

© Irene Yates
www.brilliantpublications.co.uk

Rhymes to learn and recite

One, two, three, four, five

One, two, three, four, five,
Once I caught a fish alive,
Six, seven, eight, nine, ten,
Then I let it go again.
Why did you let it go?
Because it bit my finger so.
Which finger did it bite?
This little finger on the right.

Peter Piper picked a peck

Peter Piper picked a peck
Of pickled pepper;
A peck of pickled pepper
Peter Piper picked.
If Peter Piper picked a peck
Of pickled pepper,
Where's the peck of pickled pepper
Peter Piper picked?

She sells sea-shells

She sells sea-shells
On the sea shore;
The shells she sells
Are sea-shells, I'm sure.
So if she shells sea-shells
On the sea shore,
I'm sure that the shells
Are sea shore shells.

If all the world were paper

If all the world were paper,
If all the sea were ink,
If all the trees were bread and cheese,
What should we have to drink?

Ride a cock-horse to Banbury Cross

Ride a cock-horse to Banbury Cross
To see a fine lady upon a white horse;
With rings on her fingers and bells on her toes
She shall have music wherever she goes.

Pussy-cat, pussy-cat

Pussy-cat, pussy-cat,
Where have you been?
I've been to London to visit the queen.
Pussy-cat, pussy-cat,
What did you there?
I frightened a little mouse under her chair!

Little Miss Muffet

Little Miss Muffet, sat on a tuffet,
Eating her curds and whey,
Along came a spider
Who sat down beside her
And frightened Miss Muffet away.

I hear thunder

I hear thunder,
I hear thunder,
Hark! Don't you?
Hark! Don't you?
Pitter patter raindrops,
Pitter patter raindrops,
I'm wet through.
So are you!

Rhymes to learn and recite

Here we go round the mulberry bush

Here we go round the mulberry bush, the
   mulberry bush, the mulberry bush;
Here we go round the mulberry bush, on
   a cold and frosty morning.

This is the way we … (*wash our hands;
   clean our teeth; march up and down;
   reach the sky, etc.*)

Twinkle, twinkle, little star

Twinkle, twinkle, little star,
How I wonder what you are,
Up above the world so high,
Like a diamond in the sky.

Hey diddle, diddle

Hey diddle, diddle,
The cat and the fiddle,
The cow jumped over the moon.
The little dog laughed
To see such fun
And the dish ran away with the spoon.

Diddle, diddle, dumpling

Diddle, diddle, dumpling,
My son John
Went to bed with his trousers on.
One stocking off and one stocking on,
Diddle, diddle, dumpling,
My son John.

Half a pound of tuppenny rice

Half a pound of tuppenny rice,
Half a pound of treacle,
Mix it up and make it nice,
Pop goes the weasel!
Up and down the City Road,
In and out the Eagle,
That's the way the money goes,
Pop goes the weasel!

It's raining, it's pouring

It's raining, it's pouring,
The old man is snoring,
He went to bed
And bumped his head
And couldn't get up in the morning!

© Irene Yates
www.brilliantpublications.co.uk

Storylines

Goldilocks and the Three Bears

One day, Goldilocks was walking through the woods when she came to a little cottage. She opened the door and went in.

In the kitchen were three bowls of porridge on the table.

Goldilocks tried the porridge in the biggest bowl. It was much too hot.

She tried the porridge in the middle-sized bowl. It was much too cold.

She tried the porridge in the smallest bowl. It was just right, so she ate it all up.

There were three chairs in the living room.

Goldilocks tried the biggest chair. It was much too hard.

She tried the middle-sized chair. It was much too soft.

She tried the smallest chair. It was just right, so she sat herself in it. But she was much too heavy and the chair broke into little pieces.

Goldilocks went upstairs. There were three beds in the bedroom.

She tried the biggest bed. It was much too high.

She tried the middle-sized bed. It was much too low.

She tried the smallest bed. It was just right, so she went fast asleep.

The three bears who lived in the cottage came home. They saw at once that something was wrong.

'Who's been eating my porridge?' growled Father Bear.
'Who's been eating my porridge?' growled Mother Bear.
'Who's been eating my porridge?' squeaked Baby Bear, 'And they've eaten it all up!'

They went into the living room.

'Who's been sitting in my chair?' growled Father Bear.
'Who's been sitting in my chair?' growled Mother Bear.
'Who's been sitting in my chair?' squeaked Baby Bear,
'And they've broken it all up!'

They went up to the bedroom.

'Who's been sleeping in my bed?' growled Father Bear.
'Who's been sleeping in my bed?' growled Mother Bear.
'Who's been sleeping in my bed?' squeaked Baby Bear, 'And she's still there!'

Then Goldilocks woke up and ran down the stairs and out of the door and off through the woods before the three bears could catch her!

© Irene Yates
www.brilliantpublications.co.uk

Rumpelstiltskin

Once upon a time there was a very silly man who had a beautiful daughter.

The father said, 'She's not just beautiful. She is so clever she can spin straw into gold.'

The King heard about the beautiful, clever daughter and had her brought to the palace.

He said, 'If she spins this straw into gold, I will marry her. But if she doesn't, she will die.'

The beautiful daughter was put into a turret with a pile of straw. She burst into tears. How could she spin gold out of straw?

Suddenly a little man appeared. 'Give me your gold ring,' he said, 'and I will spin the straw into gold for you.'

The next day the King was so pleased about the gold, he decided he wanted some more. 'You have to do it again tonight,' he said to the beautiful daughter, 'to prove it wasn't a trick.'

When the daughter cried again, the little man appeared. 'I'll spin the straw into gold,' he said, 'if you give me your beautiful necklace.' So she did.

Of course, the greedy King wanted more gold, so that night the beautiful daughter was shut up in a room full of straw.

She cried and cried and cried. The little man appeared. But the beautiful daughter had nothing left to give him.

'That's all right,' said the little man, 'when you are Queen I will have your first baby for my own.'

The beautiful daughter was so frightened, she agreed.

The next morning, there was so much gold, the King said, 'Start the wedding celebrations right away!' and the beautiful daughter became his Queen.
After a year, the Queen had a lovely baby girl of her own. She'd forgotten all about the little man, but one night he appeared. 'I've come to collect the baby,' he said, 'just as you promised.'

'No,' cried the Queen. 'I'll give you anything you want, but not my baby!'

The little man laughed. 'If you can guess my name before three nights have passed, I won't take your baby. But if you can't – the baby will be mine!'

On the next two nights, the Queen guessed every name she could think of but none of them was the name of the little man.

On the third day, one of the King's soldiers came to the Queen. He said, 'I saw a funny little man in the woods. He was dancing and singing. He sang, '*The Queen will never win my game, for Rumpelstiltskin is my name!*'

When the little man came that night, the Queen said, 'Is your name Hurly Burly?'

'No,' chuckled the little man.

'Is it Humpelby Bumpelby?'

'No,' chuckled the little man, rubbing his hands together gleefully.

'Is it – Rumpelstiltskin?' asked the Queen.

The little man turned red with anger and he stamped his feet so hard that he fell right through the floor of the palace.

And the Queen lived happily ever after.

Communication and Language with Literacy

© Irene Yates
www.brilliantpublications.co.uk

The Three Billy Goats Gruff

Three billy goats gruff lived in a field. They wanted to cross to the other side, to eat the best grass. But a troll lived under the bridge and if they crossed they knew he would try to eat them up.

The smallest billy goat gruff was first to cross the bridge. Trip, trap, trip, trap. The troll jumped up and said, 'Who's that crossing my bridge? I'm going to eat you up!'

The smallest billy goat said, 'Please don't eat me. My brother is bigger then me and he's coming next.' So the troll let him pass.

The middle-sized billy goat gruff was next to cross the bridge. Trip, trap, trip, trap. The troll jumped up and said, 'Who's that crossing my bridge? I'm going to eat you up!'

The middle-sized billy goat said, 'Please don't eat me. My brother is bigger then me and he's coming next.' So the troll let him pass.

Then it was the big billy goat gruff's turn to cross the bridge. Trip, trap, trip, trap. The troll jumped up and said, 'Who's that crossing my bridge? I'm going to eat you up!'

'Oh, no you're not!' cried the big billy goat and he put down his horns and tossed the troll into the air.

The troll fell into the water with a splash and the three billy goats gruff happily munched away on the other side of the river.

The Three Little Pigs

Once upon a time there were three little pigs who set off into the wide world together. They met a farmer carrying a bale of straw. The first pig said, 'I could build a house with that.' So he bought the straw and started to build a house.

The other two pigs went on. They met a woodcutter carrying a bundle of sticks. The second pig said, 'I could build a house with those.' So he bought the sticks and started to build a house.

The third pig went on. He met a workman pushing a barrow full of bricks. He said, 'I could build a house with those.' So he bought the bricks and started to build a house.

One night, the first pig was asleep in his house of straw, when a wolf came by. 'Little pig, little pig, let me in,' called the wolf. 'No, no, no, by the hair on my chinny, chin, chin, I will not let you in!' cried the pig.

'Then I'll huff and I'll puff and I'll blow your house down!' cried the wolf. And he did.

The first little pig ran to the second little pig's house of sticks.

The next night the two pigs were asleep in the house of sticks, when the wolf came by. 'Little pigs, little pigs, let me in,' called the wolf.
'No, no, no, by the hair on my chinny, chin, chin, we will not let you in!' cried the pigs.

'Then I'll huff and I'll puff and I'll blow your house down!' cried the wolf. And he did.

The little pigs ran to the third little pig's house of bricks.

The next night the three pigs were asleep in the house of bricks, when the wolf came by. 'Little pigs, little pigs, let me in,' called the wolf.
No, no, no, by the hair on my chinny, chin,

© Irene Yates
www.brilliantpublications.co.uk

The Gingerbread Man

chin, I will not let you in!' cried the pigs. 'Then I'll huff and I'll puff and I'll blow your house down!' cried the wolf. And he huffed and he puffed but he could not blow the house down.

The wolf was so angry, he said, 'If you don't let me in, I'm going to climb down the chimney!'

But the third little pig was much cleverer than the wolf. Quickly he put a pot of water on to the fire and when the wolf came down the chimney, splash! He went into the pot, and that was the end of him!

Once upon a time there lived a little old man and a little old woman, in the country. One day the little old lady had some gingerbread mixture left over.

'I'll make a little gingerbread man,' she said to herself.

She cut out the shape of a gingerbread man. She made him eyes and three buttons out of raisins. Then she popped him in the oven to bake.

The old woman heard a sound coming from the oven. She opened the door slowly. The little gingerbread man jumped up from the oven and ran out through the kitchen door. 'Come back!' shouted the old woman.

Her husband began to run after her and the gingerbread man. 'Come back,' he shouted.

But the gingerbread man called over his shoulder, 'Run, run, as fast as you can. You can't catch me, I'm the gingerbread man!'

He ran out of the gate and past a cow who was chewing grass. 'Come back!' cried the cow, and she joined in the chase.

But the gingerbread man kept on running. 'The little old woman and the little old man couldn't catch me. And neither will you! Run, run, as fast as you can. You can't catch me, I'm the gingerbread man!'

In the next field was a horse, eating hay. 'Come back!' cried the horse, and he joined in the chase.
But the gingerbread man kept on running. 'The little old woman and the little old man and the cow couldn't catch me. And neither will you! Run, run, as fast as you can. You can't catch me, I'm the gingerbread man!'

On the gate, perched a rooster, eating grain. 'Come back!' cried the rooster, and he joined in the chase.

Communication and Language with Literacy

© Irene Yates
www.brilliantpublications.co.uk

But the gingerbread man kept on running. 'The little old woman and the little old man and the cow and the horse couldn't catch me. And neither will you! Run, run, as fast as you can. You can't catch me, I'm the gingerbread man!'

In the yard, was a pig, eating slop. 'Come back!' cried the pig, and he joined in the chase.

But the gingerbread man kept on running. 'The little old woman and the little old man and the cow and the horse and the rooster couldn't catch me. And neither will you! Run, run, as fast as you can. You can't catch me, I'm the gingerbread man!'

At the end of the next field, the gingerbread man came to a wide river. He had to stop because, although he could run, he didn't know how to swim.

A big, red fox sat nearby. 'Can I help you?' said the fox. 'Just jump on my back and I'll take you across the river.'

So the gingerbread man jumped on to the fox's back. The fox slid into the river and began to swim across.

'The water is getting deeper,' said the fox. 'Climb on my head to keep yourself dry.'

So the gingerbread man did, and the fox swam on.

'The water is getting even deeper,' said the fox. 'Climb on to my nose to keep yourself dry.'

But as soon as the gingerbread man climbed on to the fox's nose, the fox threw up his head and the gingerbread man flew up into the air. Then down he fell, right into the fox's mouth. 'Snap! Snap!' went the fox.

And the gingerbread man was gone.

Characteristics of Effective Learning

Throughout all activities, practitioners need to be aware of the four themes of the Early Years Foundation Stage. Every child must be considered a *unique child* and given opportunities to form *positive relationships* within an enabling environment in order to make progress in *learning and development* in each of the prime and specific areas.

In addition to the *Learning Objectives and Early Learning Goals* listed for each activity, practitioners will seek always to encourage and observe the following *Characteristics of Effective Learning*.

Playing and Exploring

Children will find out and explore by showing curiosity and developing particular interests, using their senses and engaging in activities. They will play with what they know, acting out their own experiences through pretending and imaginative role play. They should be willing to 'have a go' by seeking new and challenging activities and being confident to try things out.

Practitioners should join in with children's play without taking over, helping, supporting and modelling ideas, challenges and risk taking and setting an example that effort and practice improves and mistakes can be learned from.

Children need flexible and stimulating resources provided within calm and ordered indoor and outdoor spaces and uninterrupted periods of time to play and explore.

Active Learning

Children will learn to become involved and concentrate on their chosen activities, displaying high levels of fascination and attention to details, maintaining focus and ignoring minor distractions. They need to develop perserverence, effort and persistence to 'keep on trying' through challenges and believe that a solution to a problem may be found or accept that an idea may not work out exactly as planned. They should enjoy meeting their own goals and challenges and be proud of their own accomplishments and achievements, without relying heavily on external praise or rewards.

Practitioners should support children in choosing their own activities, methods, plans and goals and talk with them about progress, challenges and successes. They may be encouraged to work together and learn from each other when appropriate. Specific praise for particular efforts, persistence, problem solving, good ideas and new skills acquired will help children to develop their own motivations.

Children should be provided with new and unusual activities that are linked to their current interests and given enough time and freedom for all to contribute and to become deeply involved.

Creating and Thinking Critcially

Children will have their own ideas, think of new ways to do things and find ways of solving problems for themselves. As they make connections and notice patterns and sequences within their experiences, they will learn to make predictions, test and develop their ideas and understand cause and effect. They will then be able to make informed decisions and plans, check and change their strategies as they work and play and eventually review their approaches and activities.

Practitioners should model thinking aloud, describing problems, remembering previous experiences, making connections, finding out and trying different ideas and approaches. If children's interests and conversations are supported, and sustained shared thinking is offered when appropriate, they will learn to use the 'plan-do-review' process effectively.

Children should always engage in activities in order to find their own ways to represent and develop their own ideas, using techniques and processes that they may learn from others. Routines should be recognizable and understandable to both children and adults, but also flexible enough to ensure that both security and independent development are available within the learning community.

Table of learning opportunities

Activity	Page no.	Communication and Language: Listening and attention	Communication and Language: Understanding	Communication and Language: Speaking	Physical Development: Moving and handling	Physical Development: Health and self-care	PSED: Self-confidence and self-awareness	PSED: Managing feelings and behaviour	PSED: Making relationships	Literacy: Reading	Literacy: Writing	Maths: Numbers	Maths: Shape, space and measures	Understanding the World: People and communities	Understanding the World: The world	Understanding the World: Technology	Expressive Arts and Design: Exploring and using media and materials	Expressive Arts and Design: Being imaginative
Face to face	15	✓																
I hear this	16	✓																
Guess what?	17	✓		✓														
What can it be?	18	✓																
What's this?	19	✓					✓											
I went on a bus …	20	✓																
Make a call	21	✓														✓		
What does this do?	22	✓														✓		
Finger rhymes	23	✓			✓					✓							✓	
Weather report	24	✓																
Taking turns	25	✓																
Make a new rhyme	26	✓								✓							✓	
All clap hands	27	✓			✓												✓	
Clapping the pattern	28	✓																
Which came next?	29	✓															✓	
Picture pairs	30	✓																
Rhyming names	31	✓																

Area	Aspect	32 Hey Diddle Diddle	33 Little Miss Muffet	34 Huff, puff	35 Act-a-story: Goldilocks	36 The Three Billy Goats Gruff	37 Run, run – The Gingerbread Man	38 Be a storyteller	39 Picture stories	40 Swapping stories	41 Simply a story	43 Making jigsaws	44 What's under here?	45 Where can Bear go?	46 What does he like?	47 Pass the toy	48 What can we do?	49 Copy me	50 Stand or move
Expressive Arts and Design	Being imaginative		✓		✓														
Expressive Arts and Design	Exploring and using media and materials	✓	✓															✓	
Understanding the World	Technology													✓					
Understanding the World	The world																		
Understanding the World	People and communities																		
Maths	Shape, space and measures														✓				
Maths	Numbers																	✓	
Literacy	Writing											✓	✓		✓				
Literacy	Reading	✓	✓									✓			✓				
Personal, Social and Emotional Development	Making relationships																		
Personal, Social and Emotional Development	Managing feelings and behaviour																		
Personal, Social and Emotional Development	Self-confidence and self-awareness																		
Physical Development	Health and self-care																		
Physical Development	Moving and handling		✓													✓			
Communication and Language	Speaking																		
Communication and Language	Understanding									✓		✓	✓	✓	✓	✓	✓		✓
Communication and Language	Listening and attention	✓	✓	✓	✓	✓	✓	✓	✓	✓	✓							✓	

Area	Aspect	51	52	53	54	55	56	57	58	59	60	62	63	64	65	66	67	68	69	70
Expressive Arts and Design	Being imaginative		✓			✓				✓						✓				✓
	Exploring and using media and materials				✓												✓			
Understanding the World	Technology																			
	The world																		✓	
	People and communities																			
Mathematics	Shape, space and measures																			
	Numbers																			
Literacy	Writing																	✓		
	Reading							✓												
Personal, Social and Emotional Development	Making relationships	✓																		
	Managing feelings and behaviour										✓									
	Self-confidence and self-awareness	✓								✓	✓				✓					
Physical Development	Health and self-care																			
	Moving and handling					✓														
Communication and Language	Speaking	✓	✓	✓		✓				✓	✓		✓	✓	✓	✓	✓	✓	✓	✓
	Understanding	✓	✓	✓	✓	✓	✓	✓	✓	✓	✓									
	Listening and attention													✓						
Activity		Build a den	Hospital area	Be a pirate	Making puppets	Sew-sew	Wordless books	Make one like it	Talking about stories	Acting stories	How would I feel?	Observe, wait and listen	Speak and listen	What is it?	Tell us about …	Make and play	Fish and chips	Collecting	What's outside?	Making stories

© Irene Yates
www.brilliantpublications.co.uk

Area	Aspect	71 Order, order	72 Right order	73 Make musical instruments	74 Dressing-up box	75 Space shuttle	76 Office centre	77 What I liked was …	78 Re-jig a familiar story	79 Building stories	80 Who shall I be?	83 Build a castle	84 Post delivery person	85 Same and different	86 Setting up a book area	87 Be a reading role model	88 Choosing books	89 Looking at books together
Expressive Arts and Design	Being imaginative				✔						✔							
	Exploring and using media and materials			✔								✔						
Understanding the World	Technology					✔	✔											
	The world																	
	People and communities												✔					
Mathematics	Shape, space and measures																	
	Numbers					✔												
Literacy	Writing					✔								✔				✔
	Reading												✔	✔	✔	✔	✔	✔
Personal, Social and Emotional Development	Making relationships																	
	Managing feelings and behaviour																	
	Self-confidence and self-awareness							✔										
Physical Development	Health and self-care																	
	Moving and handling																	
Communication and Language	Speaking	✔	✔	✔	✔	✔	✔	✔	✔		✔	✔						
	Understanding						✔		✔			✔						
	Listening and attention																✔	

Area	Aspect	90 Which book?	91 Time to read	92 Reading together	93 Sharing books	94 Read it with feeling	95 Understanding stories	96 Book know-how	97 Library visit	98 Reading moments	99 Sharing a book	100 Whole words	101 Look for words	102 Sound box	103 Letter train	104 Guess what it is	105 Silly words	106 Match the letter	107 Misfit words	108 Pocket letters
Expressive Arts and Design	Being imaginative																			
	Exploring and using media and materials																			
Understanding the World	Technology																			
	The world																			
	People and communities																			
Mathematics	Shape, space and measures																			
	Numbers																			
Literacy	Writing						✓								✓					✓
	Reading	✓	✓	✓	✓	✓	✓	✓	✓	✓	✓	✓	✓	✓	✓	✓	✓	✓	✓	✓
Personal, Social and Emotional Development	Making relationships														✓					
	Managing feelings and behaviour																			
	Self-confidence and self-awareness																			
Physical Development	Health and self-care																			
	Moving and handling																			
Communication and Language	Speaking																			
	Understanding															✓				
	Listening and attention				✓	✓					✓									

Activity	Page no.	Being imaginative	Exploring and using media and materials	Technology	The world	People and communities	Shape, space and measures	Numbers	Writing	Reading	Making relationships	Managing feelings and behaviour	Self-confidence and self-awareness	Health and self-care	Moving and handling	Speaking	Understanding	Listening and attention
I can …	109								✔	✔								
Silly sentences	110								✔	✔								
Echoes	111									✔								
Naming names	112									✔								
Know-a-name	113								✔	✔								
Chant a story	114								✔	✔								
Make a necklace	115								✔	✔					✔			
Print walk	116								✔	✔								
Shopping trip	117									✔								
Re-tell a story	118									✔						✔		
Book words	119								✔	✔								
Feel free book	120		✔							✔					✔			
Print a book	121			✔					✔	✔								
Send an e-mail	122			✔					✔									
Do these words rhyme?	125								✔									
Make a sound book	126								✔	✔								
I-spy alphabet book	127								✔	✔								
Scribble, scribble	128								✔						✔			
Controlled scribble	129								✔						✔			

Area	Aspect	Special writing (130)	Over-copying (131)	Copy-writing (132)	Marks for meaning (133)	Modelling writing (134)	Sand-writing (135)	Sky-writing (136)	Chalk-a-line (137)	Matching shapes (138)	Write it right! (139)	This is me (140)	Signing in (141)	Writing notes (142)	Watch out! (143)	Colour words (144)	Make a card (145)	Have a go (146)	Design a cover (147)	Easy peasy book (148)	A simple flap book (149)
Expressive Arts and Design	Being imaginative																				
	Exploring and using media and materials																		✓		
Understanding the World	Technology																	✓			
	The world																				
	People and communities															✓					
Mathematics	Shape, space and measures									✓											
	Numbers								✓												
Literacy	Writing	✓	✓	✓	✓	✓	✓	✓	✓	✓	✓	✓	✓	✓	✓	✓	✓	✓	✓	✓	✓
	Reading		✓		✓							✓								✓	✓
Personal, Social and Emotional Development	Making relationships																				
	Managing feelings and behaviour																				
	Self-confidence and self-awareness													✓							
Physical Development	Health and self-care																				
	Moving and handling		✓				✓	✓	✓		✓	✓				✓	✓				✓
Communication and Language	Speaking									✓							✓				
	Understanding																				
	Listening and attention																				

196   **Communication and Language with Literacy**

Area	Aspect	150	151	152	153	154	155	156	157	158	159	160	161	162	163	164	165	166	167
Expressive Arts and Design	Being imaginative		✓					✓			✓	✓		✓	✓				
	Exploring and using media and materials	✓	✓				✓												
Understanding the World	Technology																✓	✓	
	The world																		
	People and communities				✓														
Mathematics	Shape, space and measures																		
	Numbers									✓									
Literacy	Writing		✓	✓	✓	✓	✓	✓	✓	✓	✓	✓	✓	✓	✓	✓	✓	✓	✓
	Reading	✓		✓										✓	✓				
Personal, Social and Emotional Development	Making relationships																		
	Managing feelings and behaviour																		
	Self-confidence and self-awareness																		
Physical Development	Health and self-care																		
	Moving and handling						✓												✓
Communication and Language	Speaking				✓	✓													
	Understanding								✓	✓				✓					
	Listening and attention																		
Page no.		150	151	152	153	154	155	156	157	158	159	160	161	162	163	164	165	166	167
Activity		More flap books	Simple pop-up books	Photo albums	Family album	Zig-zag book	Going for a walk book	Treasure map	Message in a bottle	Make a restaurant	Set up a fish and chip shop	Wild animal park	Transport	Write me a letter	Send a letter	Taking messages	Making labels	What's your favourite …?	Keeping a writing record

Index of topics

Lightning Source UK Ltd.
Milton Keynes UK
UKOW07f2112210715

255589UK00001B/1/P